AF444233

What Do I Feed the Birds?

Easy Ways to Attract Our Feathered Friends

Kelley Manson

Redpoll Publishing May 2025

Copyright @ 2025 Kelley Manson

All photos taken by the author

Redpoll Publishing May 2025

Printed in the United States

All rights reserved. No part of this publication may be reproduced, copied, or utilized in any form, digital, electronic or mechanical, without permission in writing from the author.

Dedication

To Mom and Dad, who always enjoyed watching the bird feeders out their living room window - especially when the chickadees and hummingbirds came.

Foreword

Kelley loves her birds, and this simple guide helps to ID who visits our backyard and what they like to eat. It's also great for children to learn how to feed the birds. Everyone should own a copy of this beautiful book!

~ Matthew A. Young

    President & Founder of The Finch Research Network (FiRN)

    Co-author of The Stokes Guide to Finches of the United States and Canada

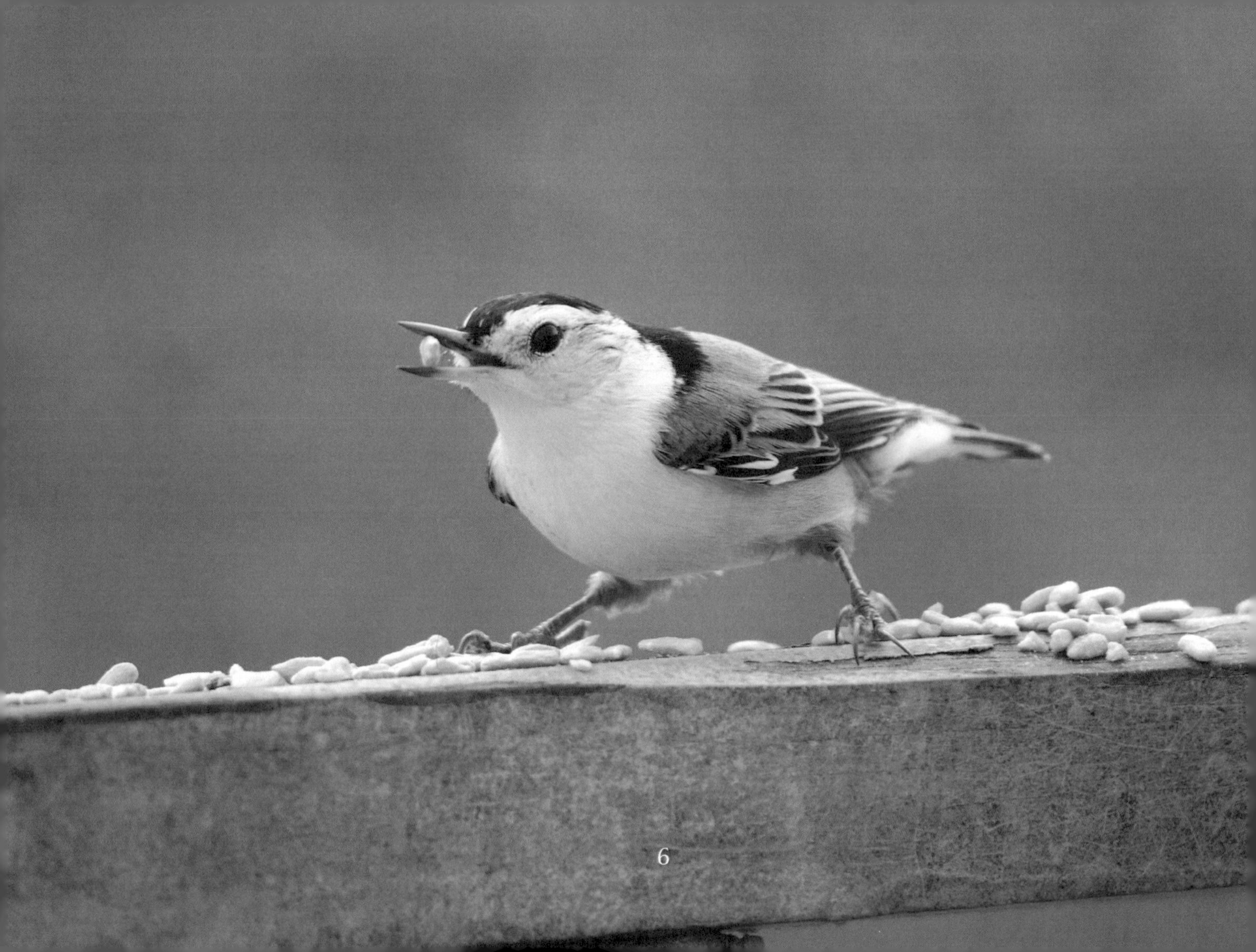

Table of Contents

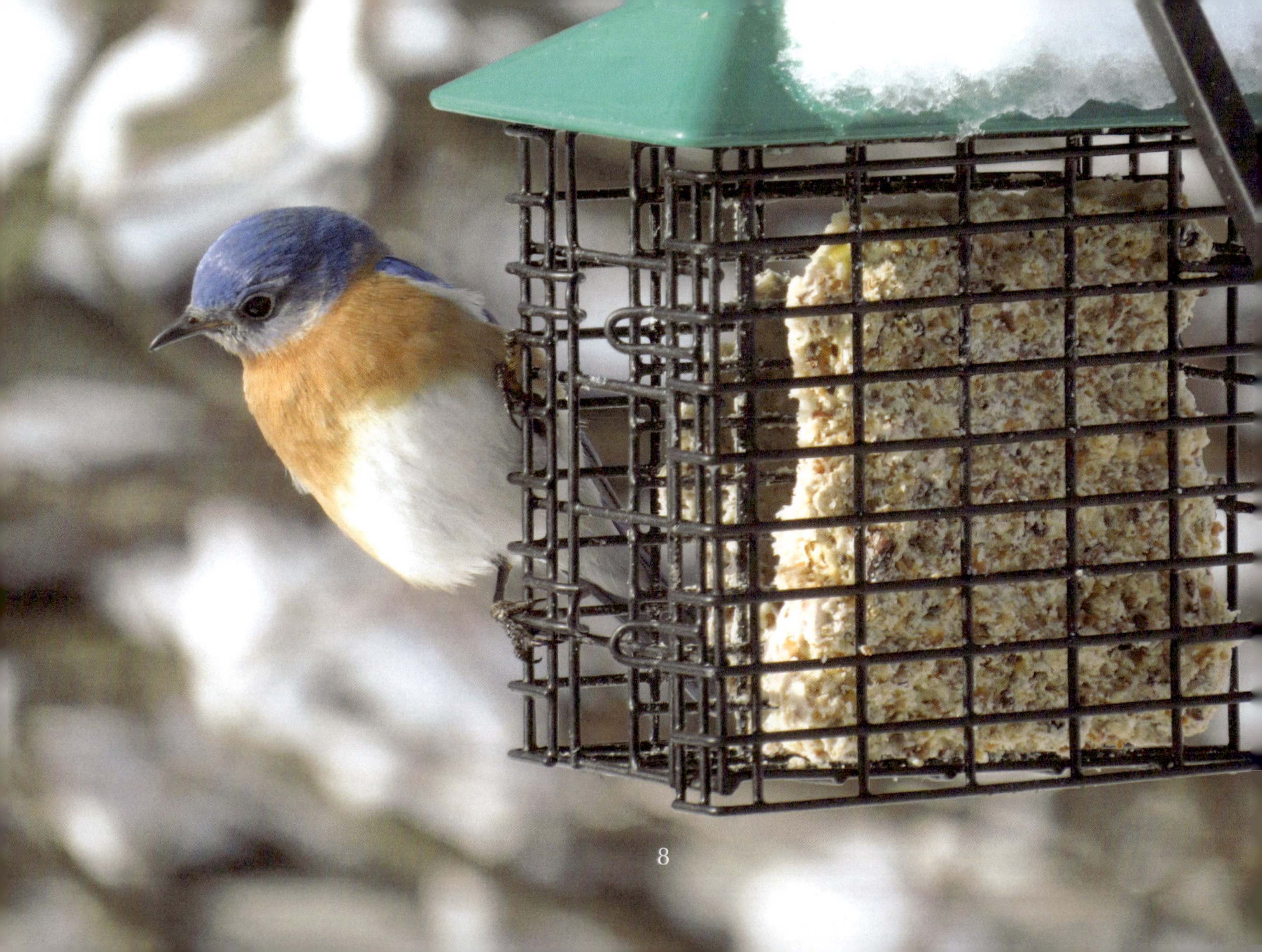

Introduction

Bird Lady. Birdwatcher. Bird nerd. Birder.

I've had a love of all things birds my entire life. Growing up in New England, I couldn't wait until wintertime when I could feed the birds and watch them up close. That excitement still exists today.

This book shows the different kinds of birdseed and other food to feed wild birds, as well as examples of photos showing the variety of birds that will come to your feeders. Bird feeding is a simple way to bring joy into our lives, while at the same time, helping our beautiful feathered friends survive and thrive.

~ Kelley

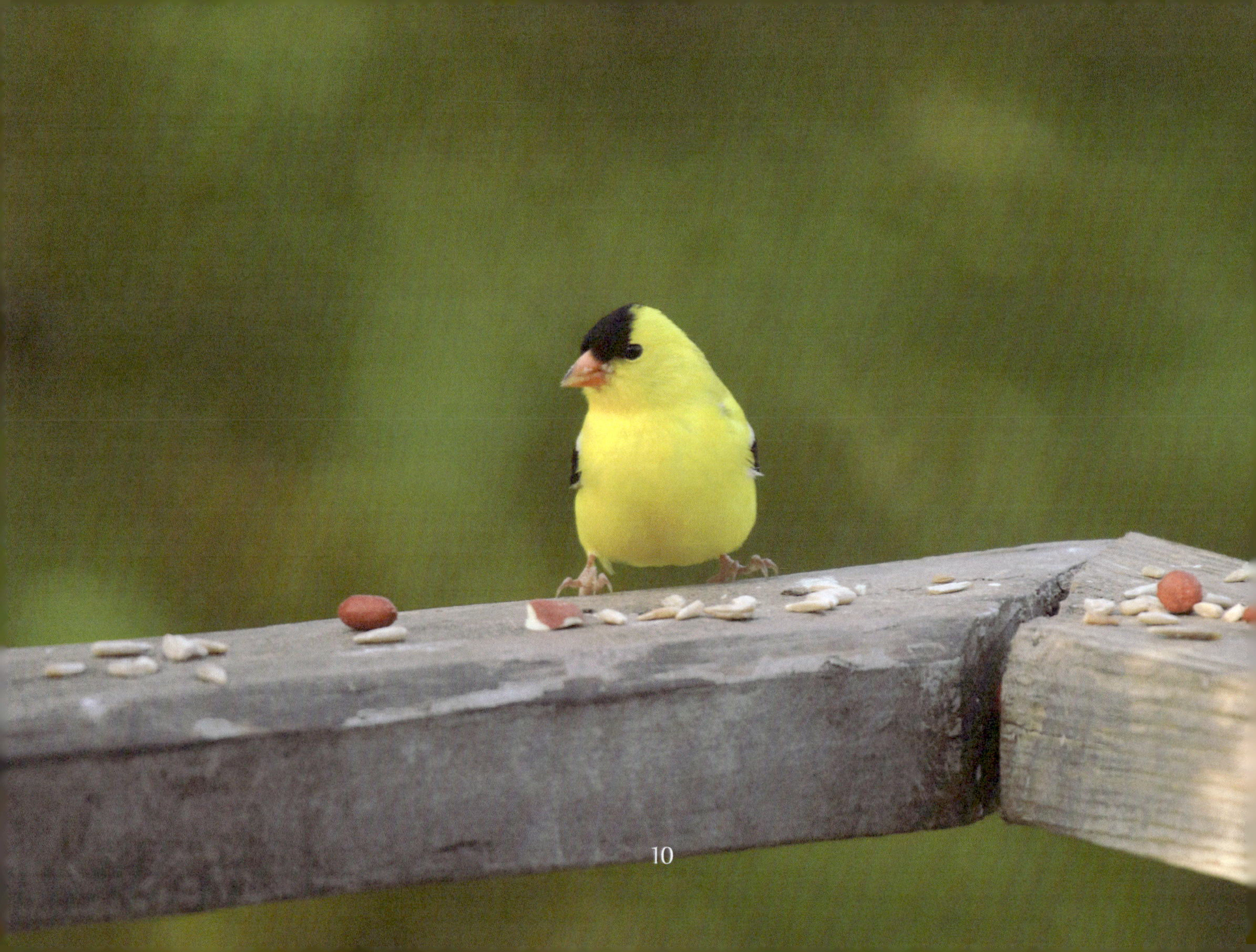

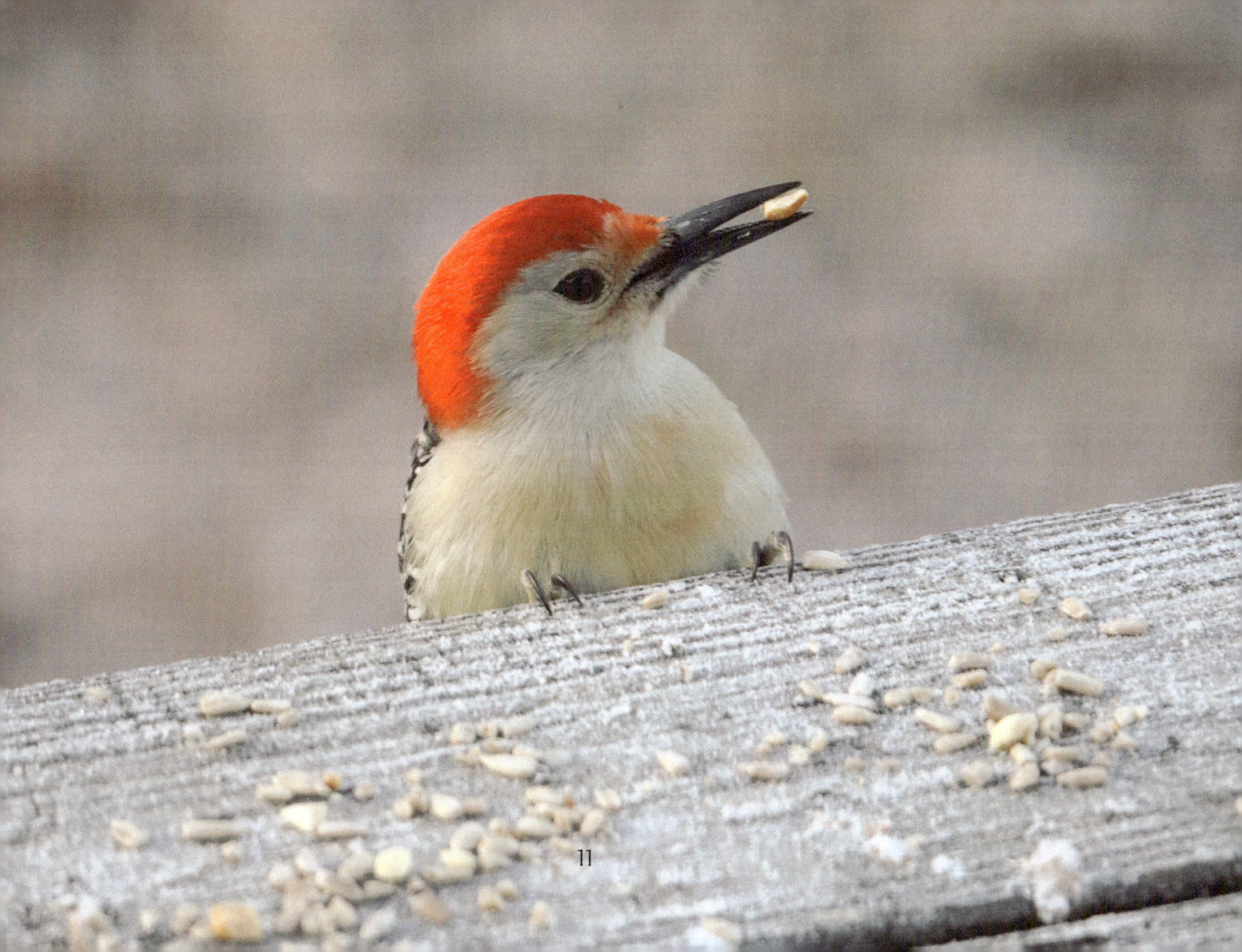

Choosing which birdseed to get can be intimidating as there are so many kinds to choose from. The best all-around choice is sunflower. Every seed-eating bird will eat sunflower seeds – black oil is small and the shell is softer to crack. Shelled (hulled) sunflower is just the inside "meat" with no shell. Some of the birds you will attract will be the Cardinal, Chickadee, Tufted Titmouse, Nuthatch, House Finch, and Carolina Wren.

Striped sunflower is larger with a harder shell, for bigger birds, attracting the Blue Jay and Evening Grosbeak.

Sunflower seeds have a high fat content which helps keep birds warm in the winter.

Black Oil   Shelled   Striped

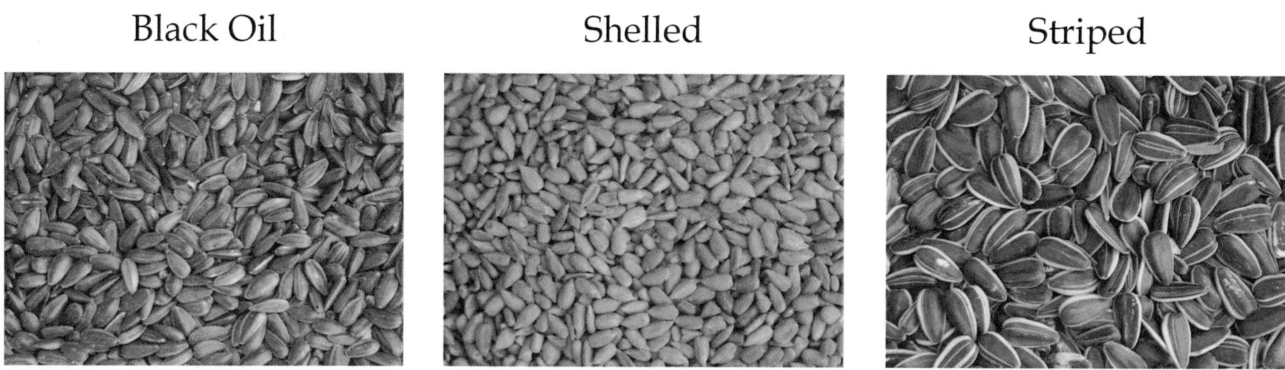

Mixed seed offers a variety to appeal to different preferences all in one bag. This is commonly thrown on the ground or used in platform feeders attracting Mourning Doves, Sparrows, Juncos, and Bluebirds.

Some mixed seed can contain black oil, millet, safflower, peanut chips, cracked corn, and dried fruit. Also, specialty "blends" and "mixes" are sold targeting favorite foods for a singular bird type like cardinals and finches.

Nyjer seed (also called thistle) is a popular standalone seed that many choose to attract the American Goldfinch as well as the Common Redpoll and Pine Siskin.

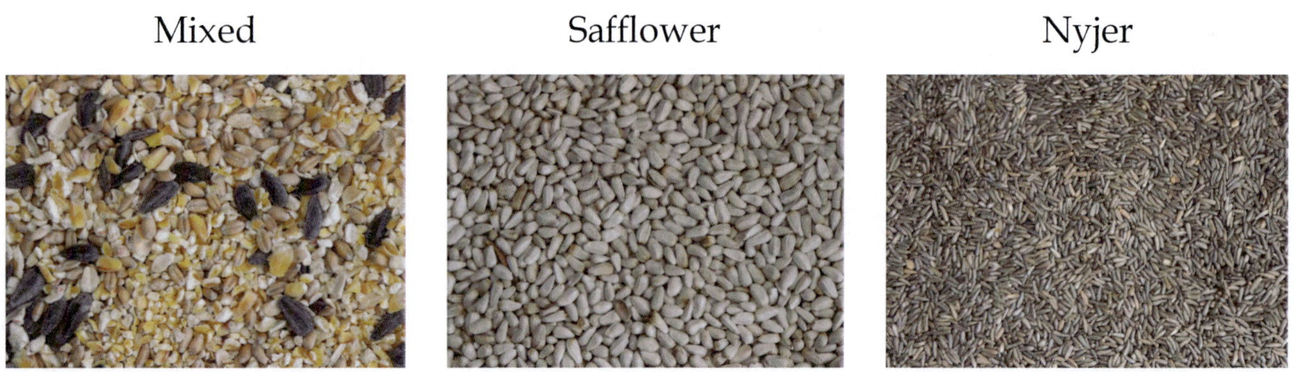

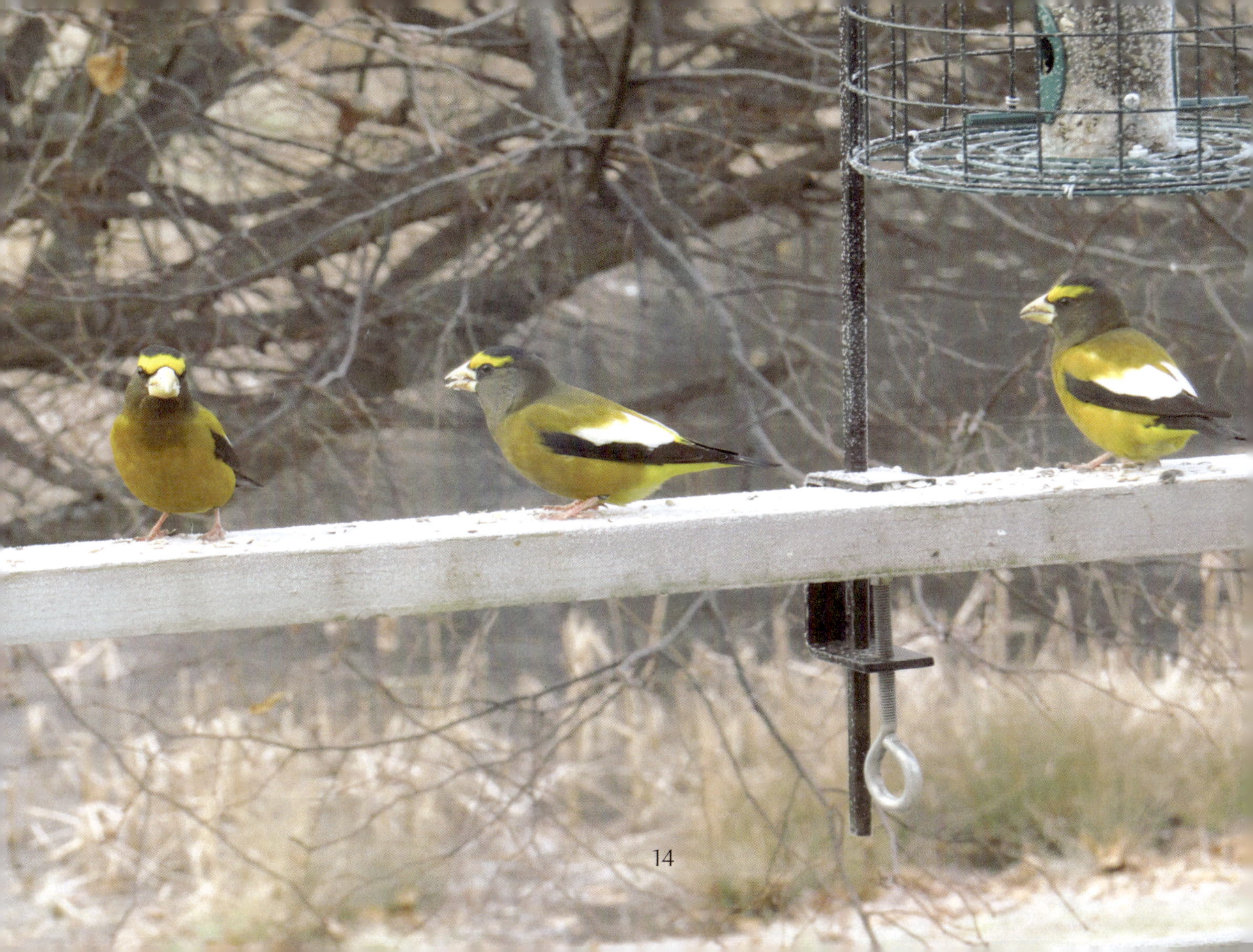

14

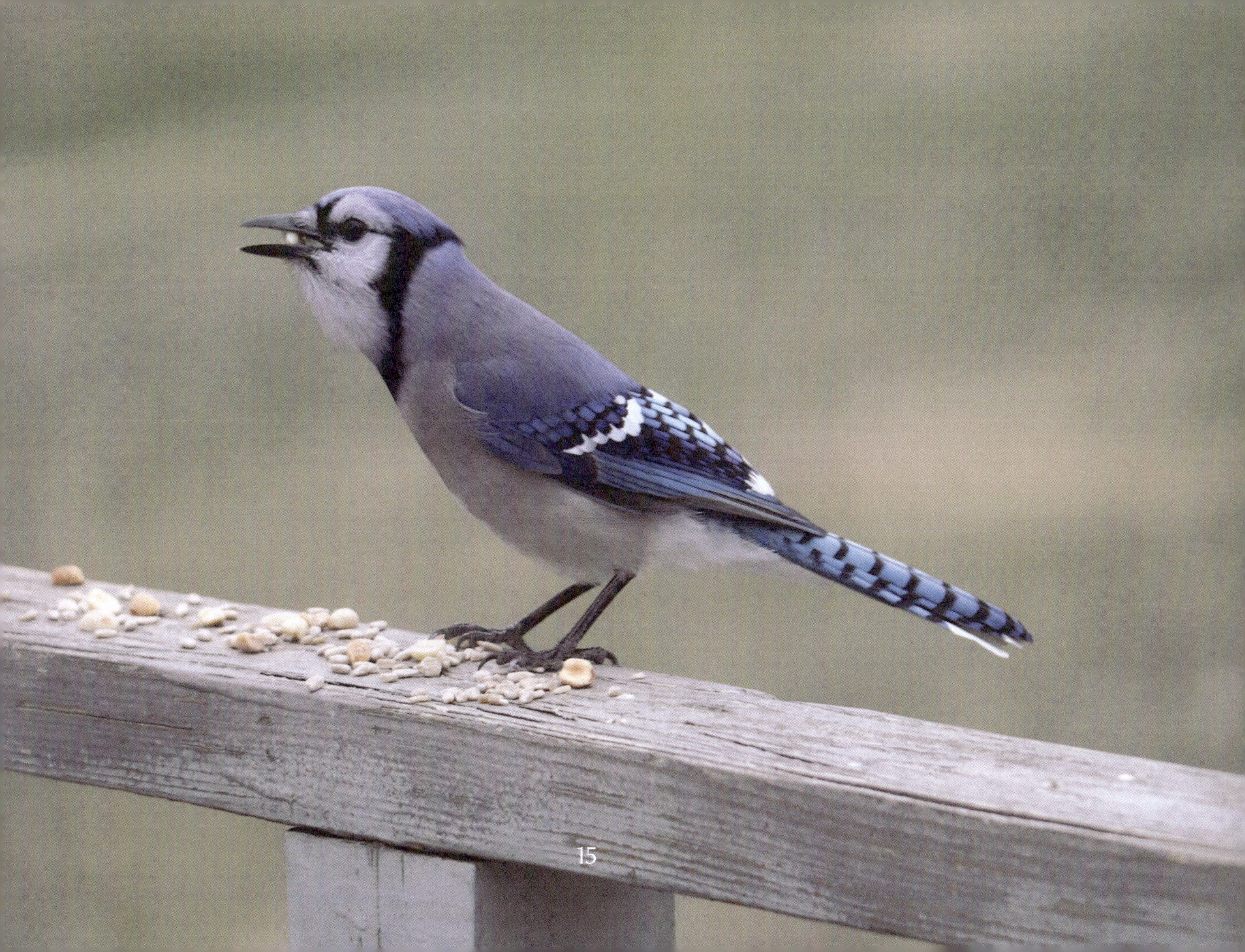

Suet is fat-based, high energy, food that birds love. It's widely sold at garden supply stores and is now commonly found in supermarkets as well.

Different kinds of seeds can be added to the suet, offering a variety of choices including sunflower, dried fruit, peanut chips, and cracked corn. It comes in a 5x5 inch square serving size to fit right into your suet feeder.

Some birds attracted are Woodpeckers, Nuthatches, and Chickadees.

Not only will suet attract birds in the winter, it's an important staple during spring migration. Along the way, flying hundreds of miles to get to their northern seasonal nesting grounds, birds are hungry and in need of calories. (Or, in general, it can be eaten all year-round).

This is a fun time to see uncommon species that normally eat bugs, grasshoppers, and flying insects. These birds will eat suet to get through until their normal food source is available. The kinds of birds you may see are the Red-winged Blackbird, Northern Flicker, Rose-breasted Grosbeak, Catbird, Baltimore Oriole, Bluebird, and early warblers.

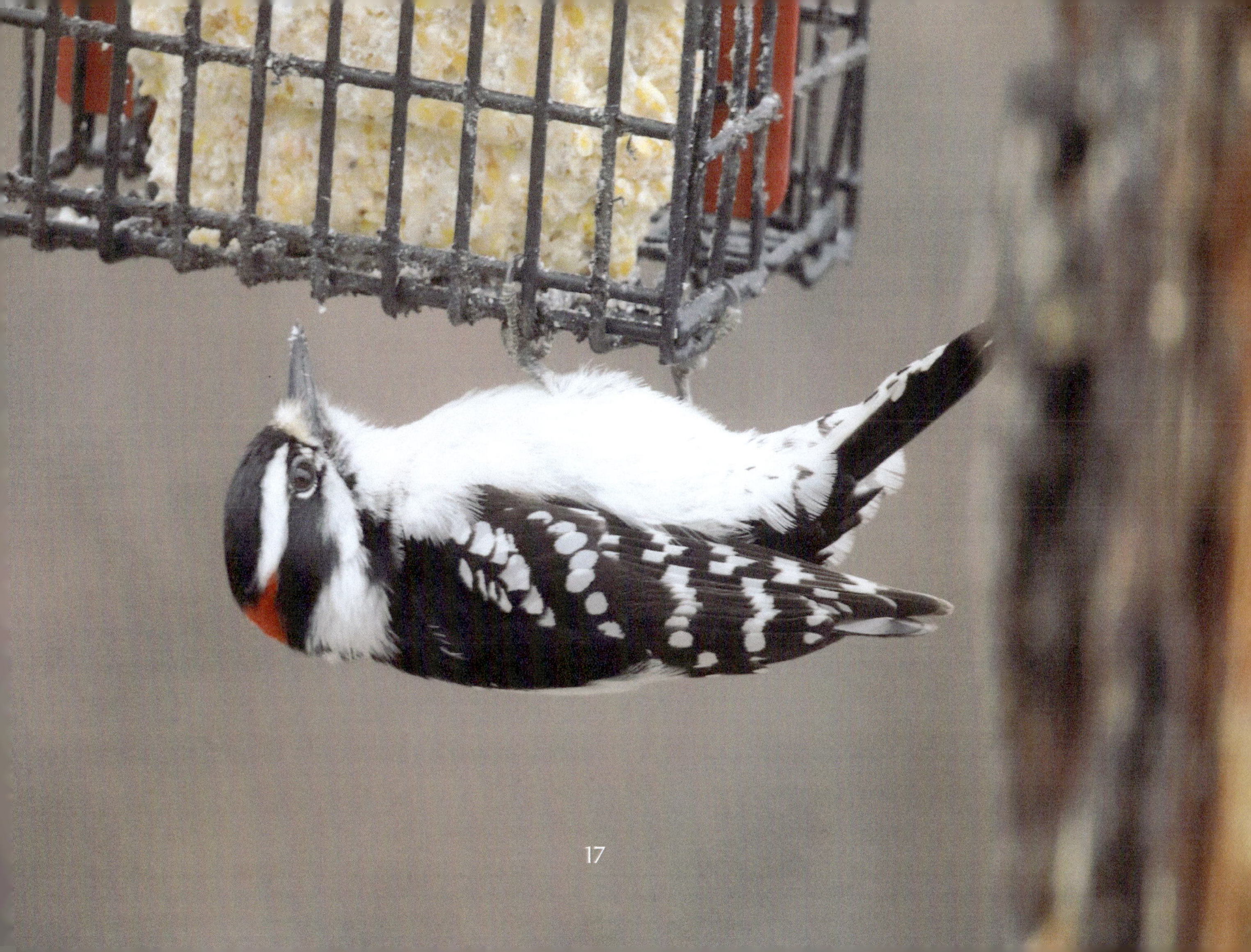

Two-Ingredient Bird Treat

2 cups of bird seed

1 cup of peanut butter

In a large bowl, thoroughly combine ingredients.

Spoon into suet feeder.

Can also take a pine cone and roll/ spoon mixture until wedged between cone layers. Tie to a tree branch or hang from a bird feeder pole.

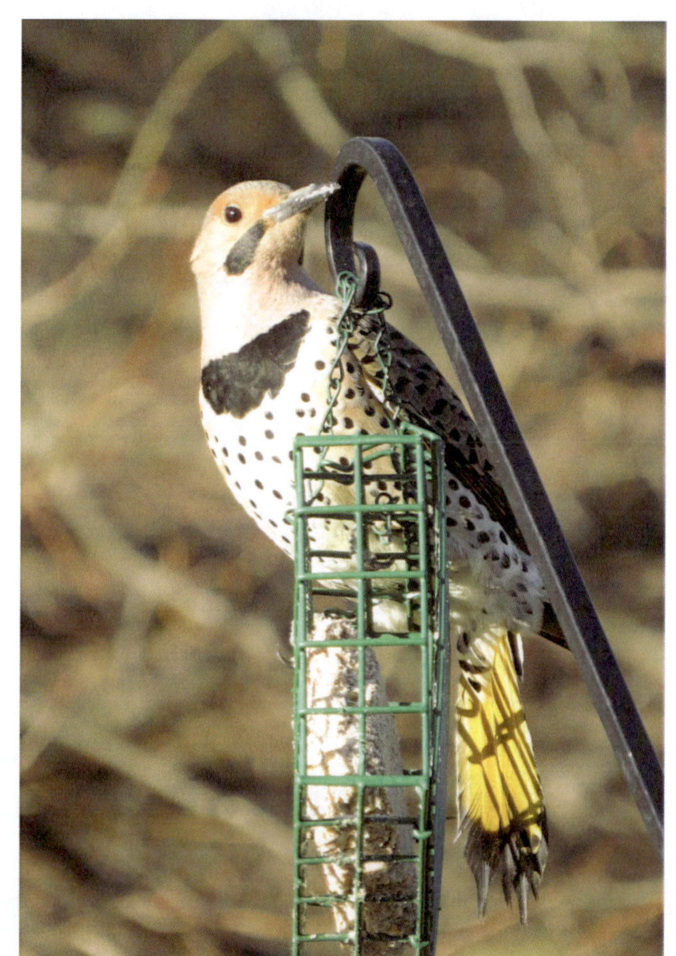

Home-made Suet

2 cups of bird seed

3/4 cup of peanut butter

1 cup of fat: shortening or drippings from cooked ground beef

1/2 cup of oats

1/4 cup of cornmeal

Optional:

1/4 cup of raisons or chopped apples

1/2 cup of chopped peanuts

Mix dry ingredients together in a bowl. Set aside.

In a separate bowl, combine the warm melted fat and peanut butter. Stir well.

Pour dry ingredients into the fat and peanut butter mixture. Combine well.

Spoon into desired containers; can use ice cube trays.

Freeze for 2 hours.

Pop mixture out of container and place in suet feeder.

Use when outside temperature is under 50 degrees

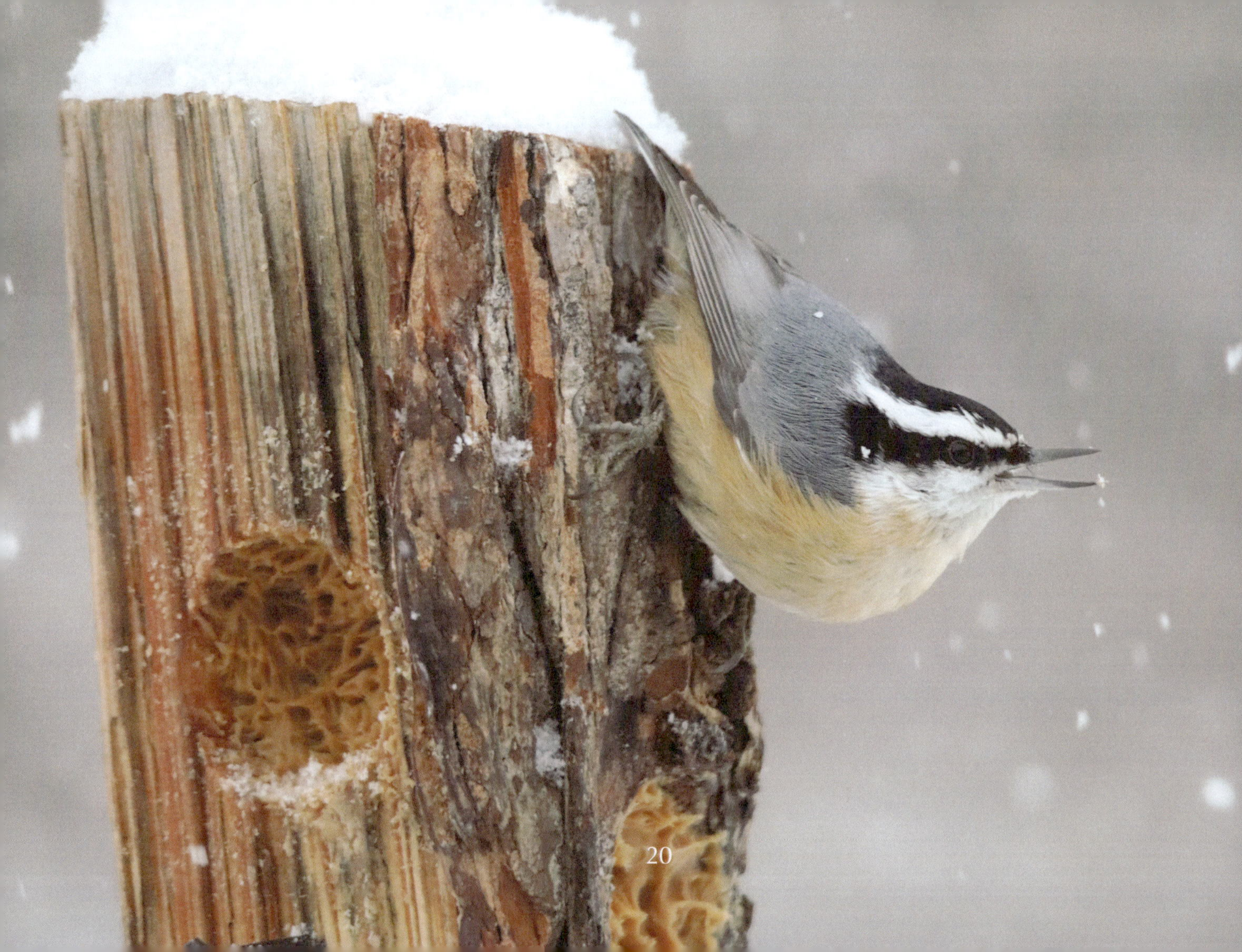

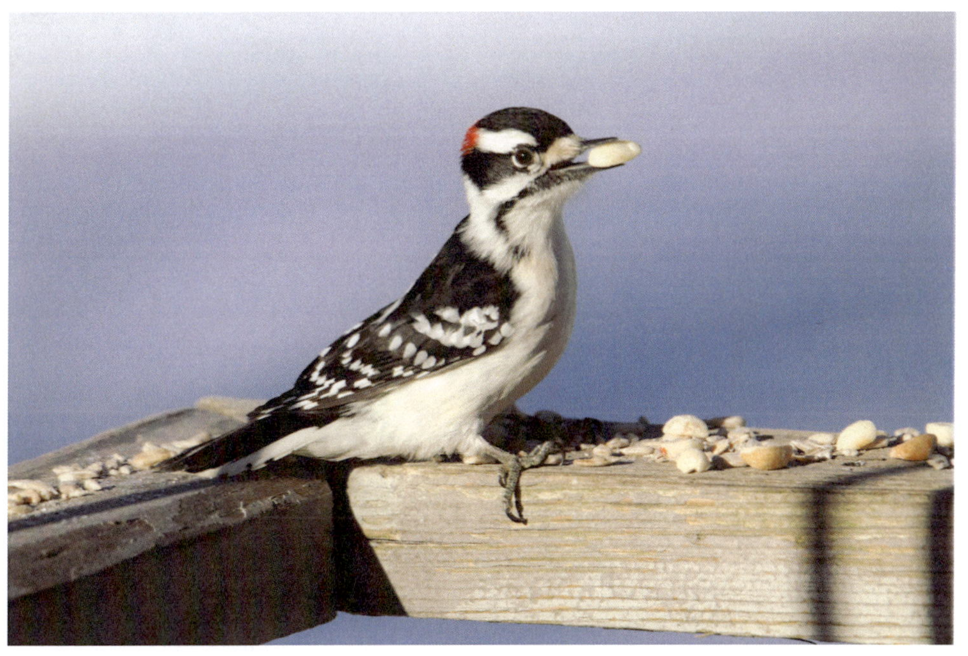

Peanuts and peanut butter are an important winter staple containing high protein and fat. This helps birds maintain their energy and body temperature.

You can purchase special feeders or just throw peanuts on the ground or deck. Peanut butter can also be spread on tree bark.

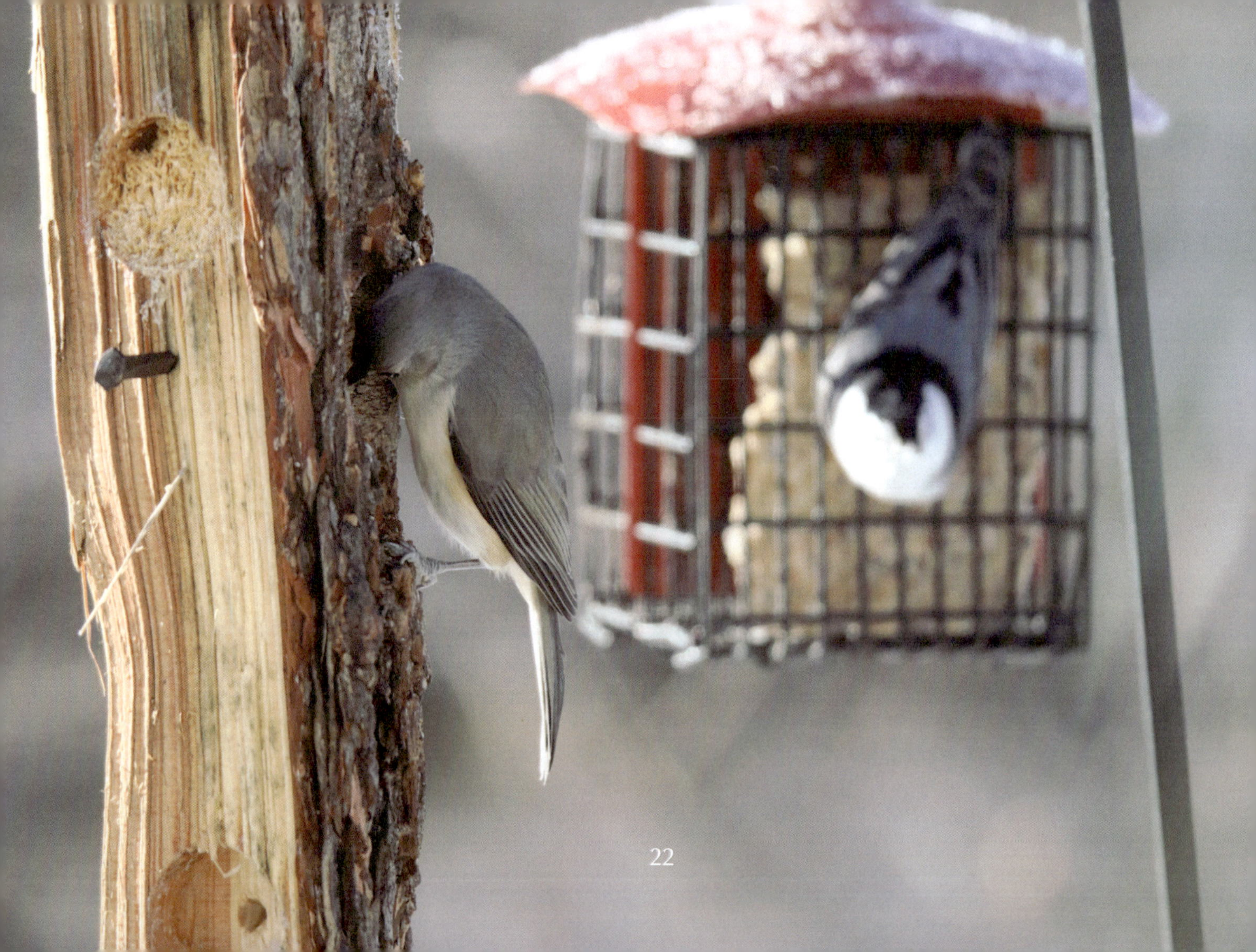

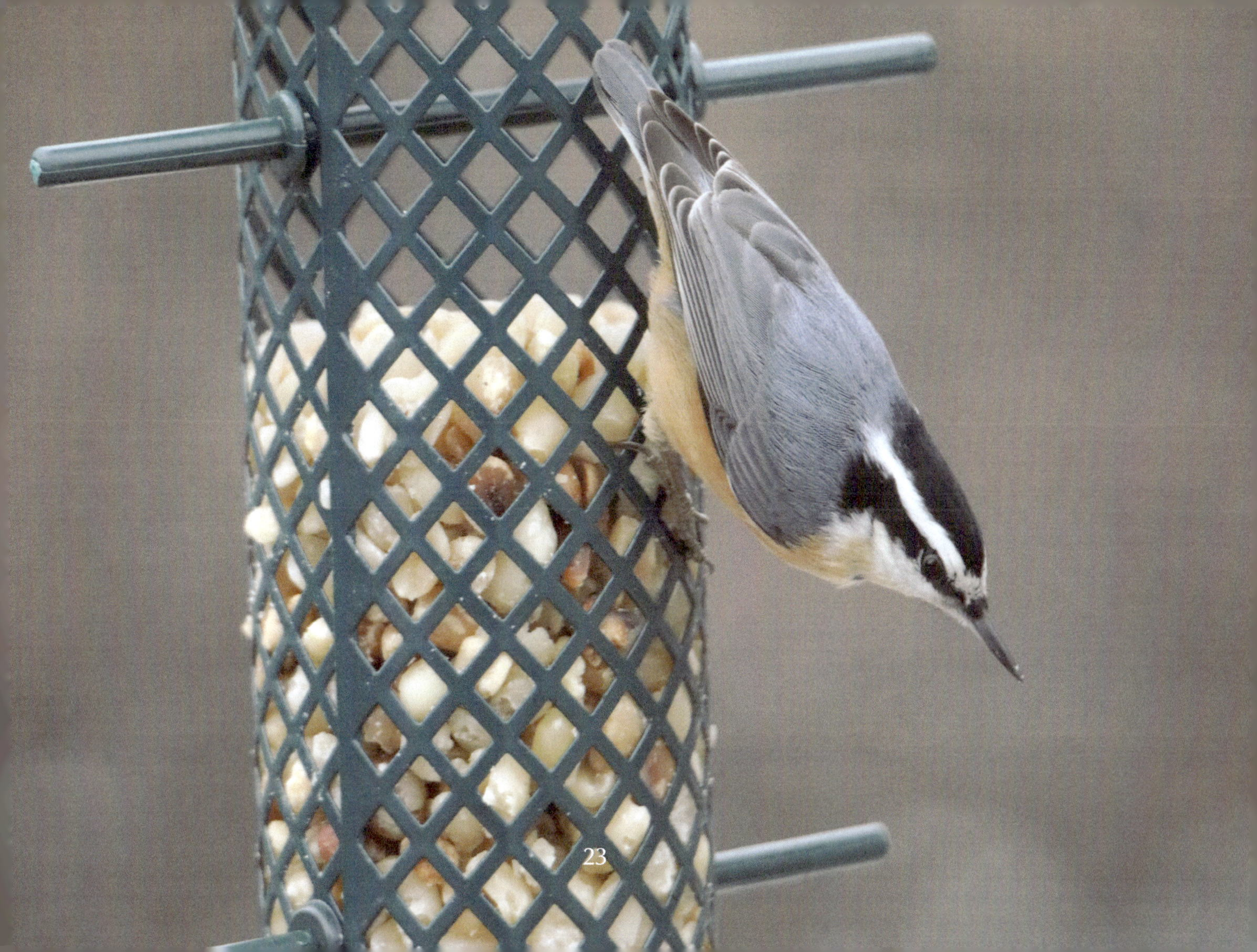

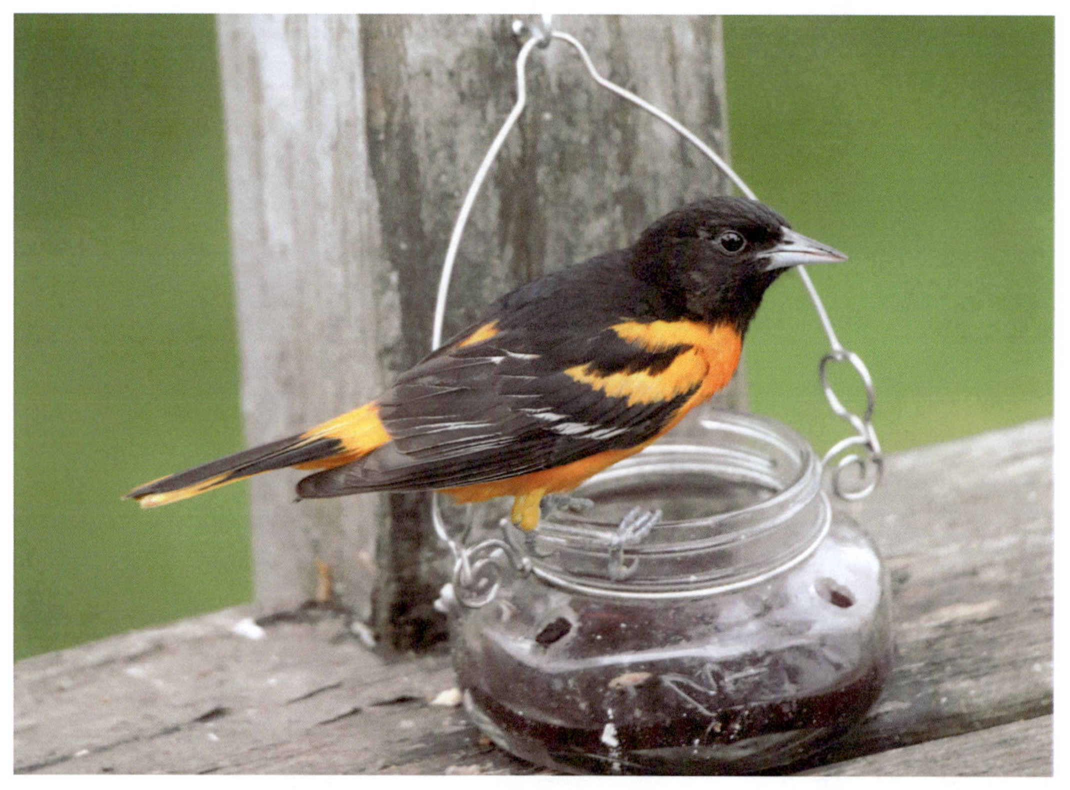

Grape jelly is a sweet treat, add some to any sturdy container or specialty feeder and birds will find it.

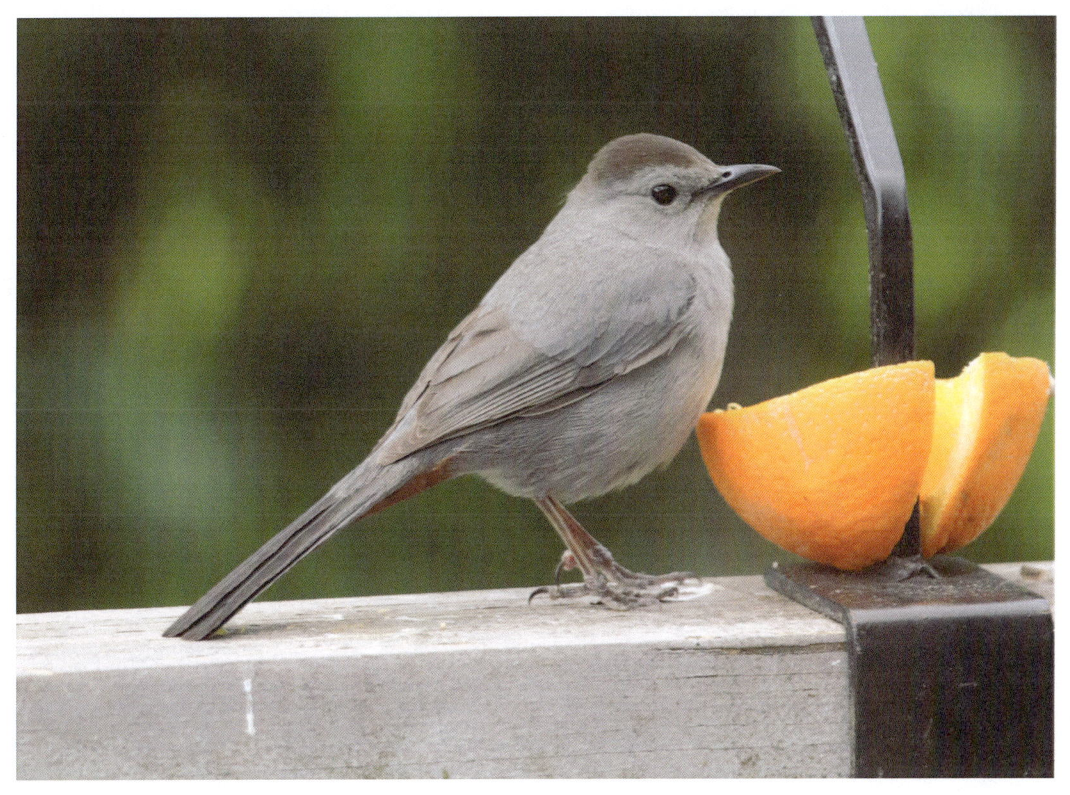

Cut up an **orange** to attract a variety of birds.

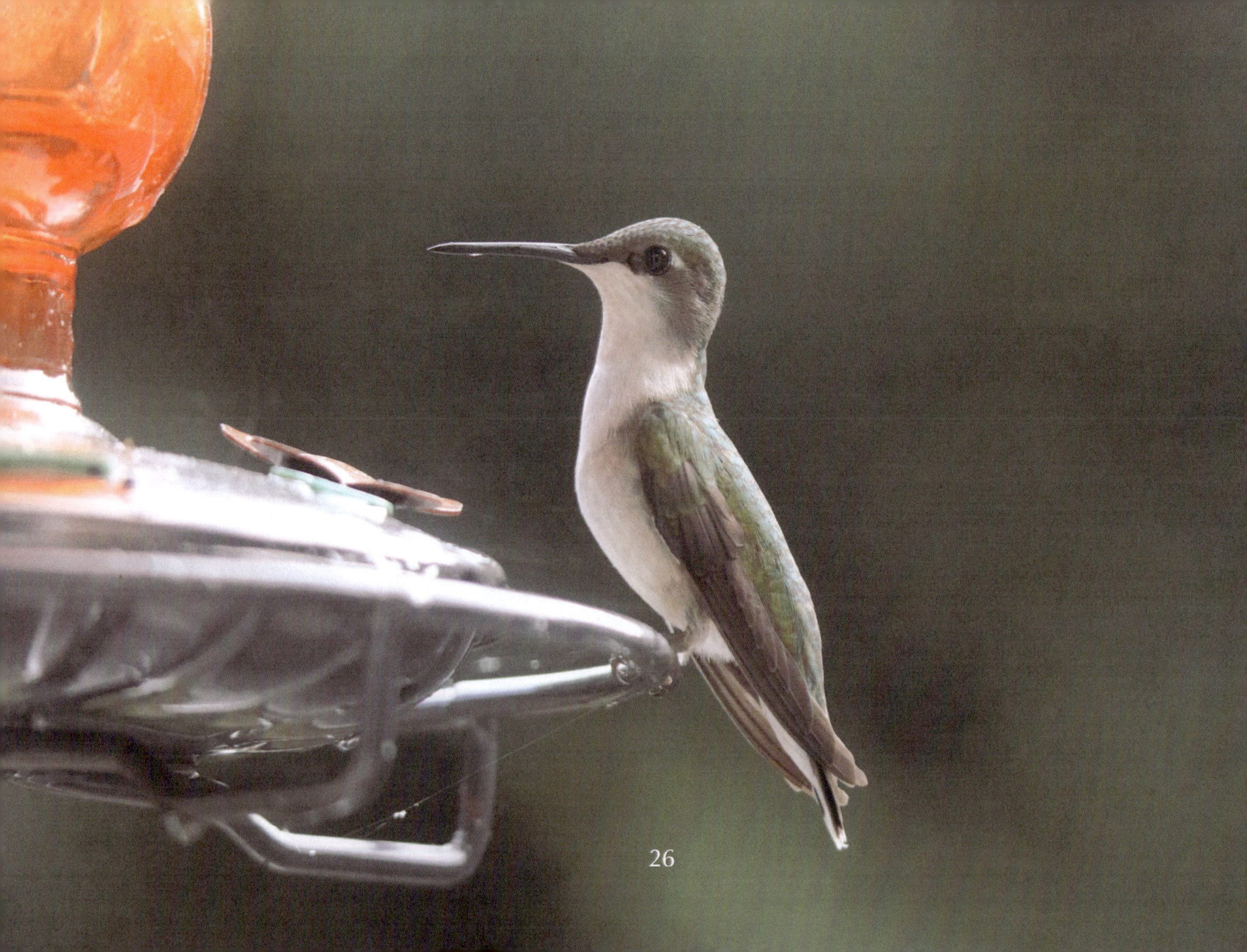

Food for Hummingbirds

Hummingbirds love sugar water. The best way to feed them is with a homemade solution.

1 cup of water (or 2 cups of water)

1/3 cup of white granular sugar (or 2/3 cup of sugar)

Mix well, stirring until the sugar dissolves.

Sugar water can also attract other birds. You may see Orioles and Rose-breasted Grosbeaks stopping for a drink.

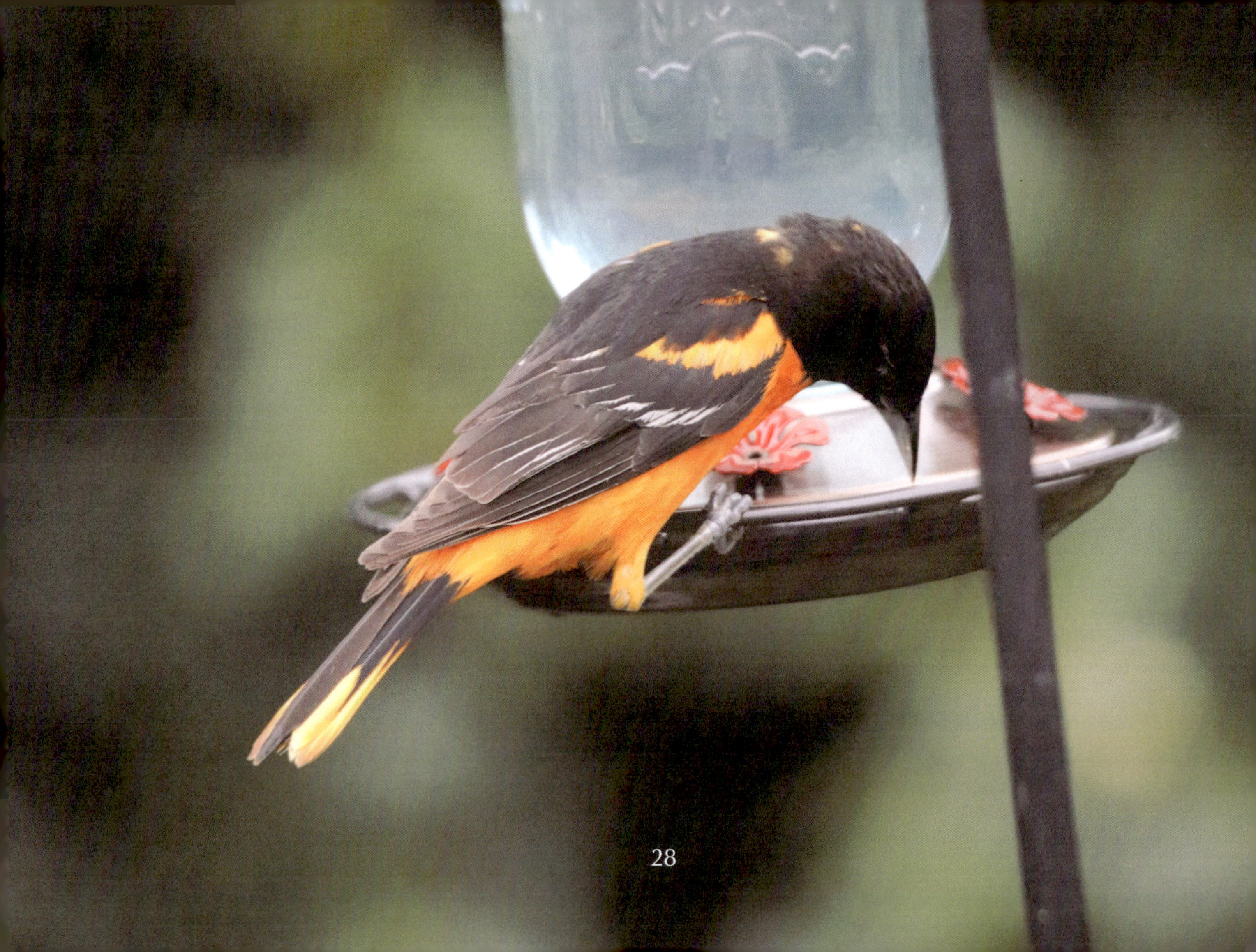

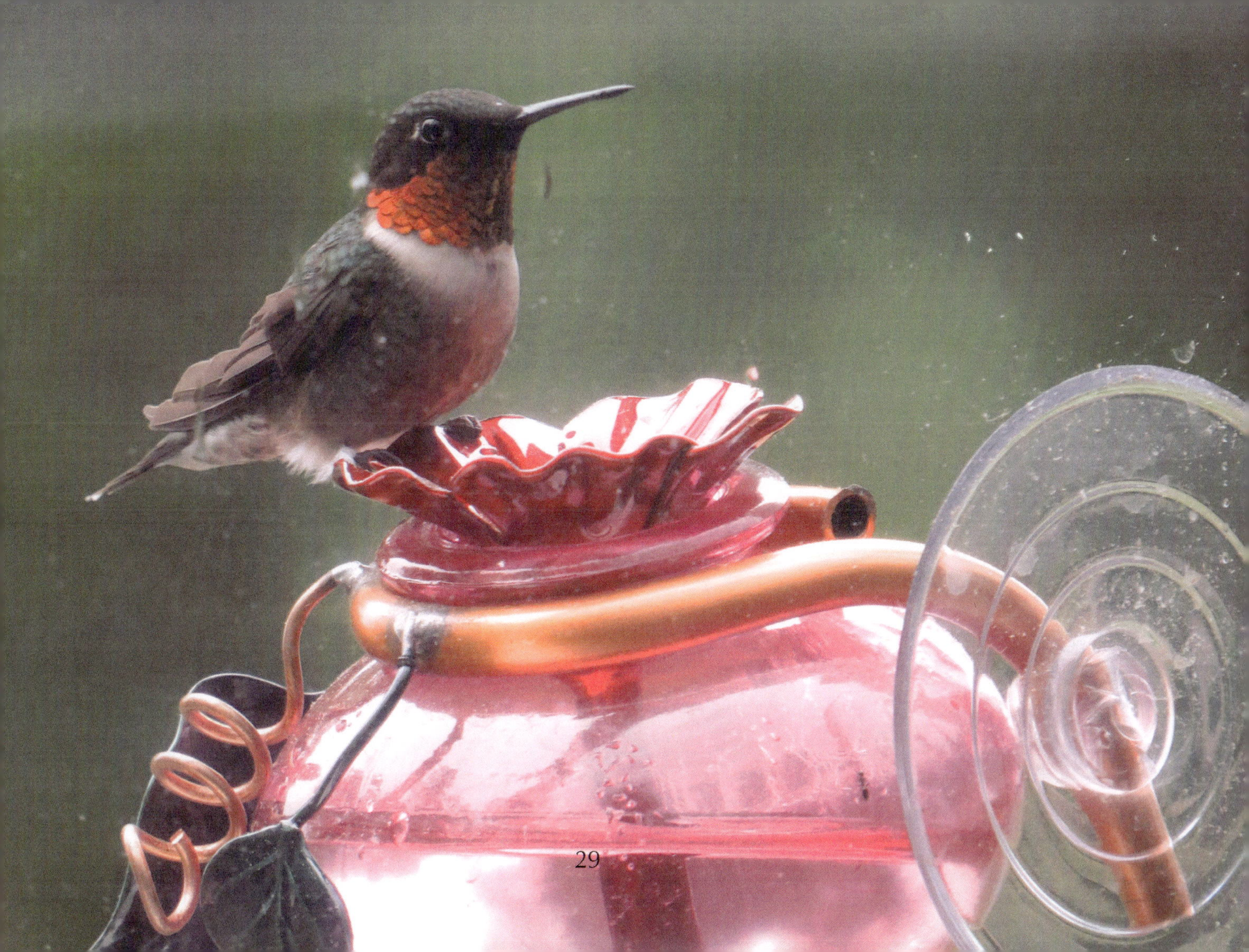

Enjoy These Birds at Your Feeders!

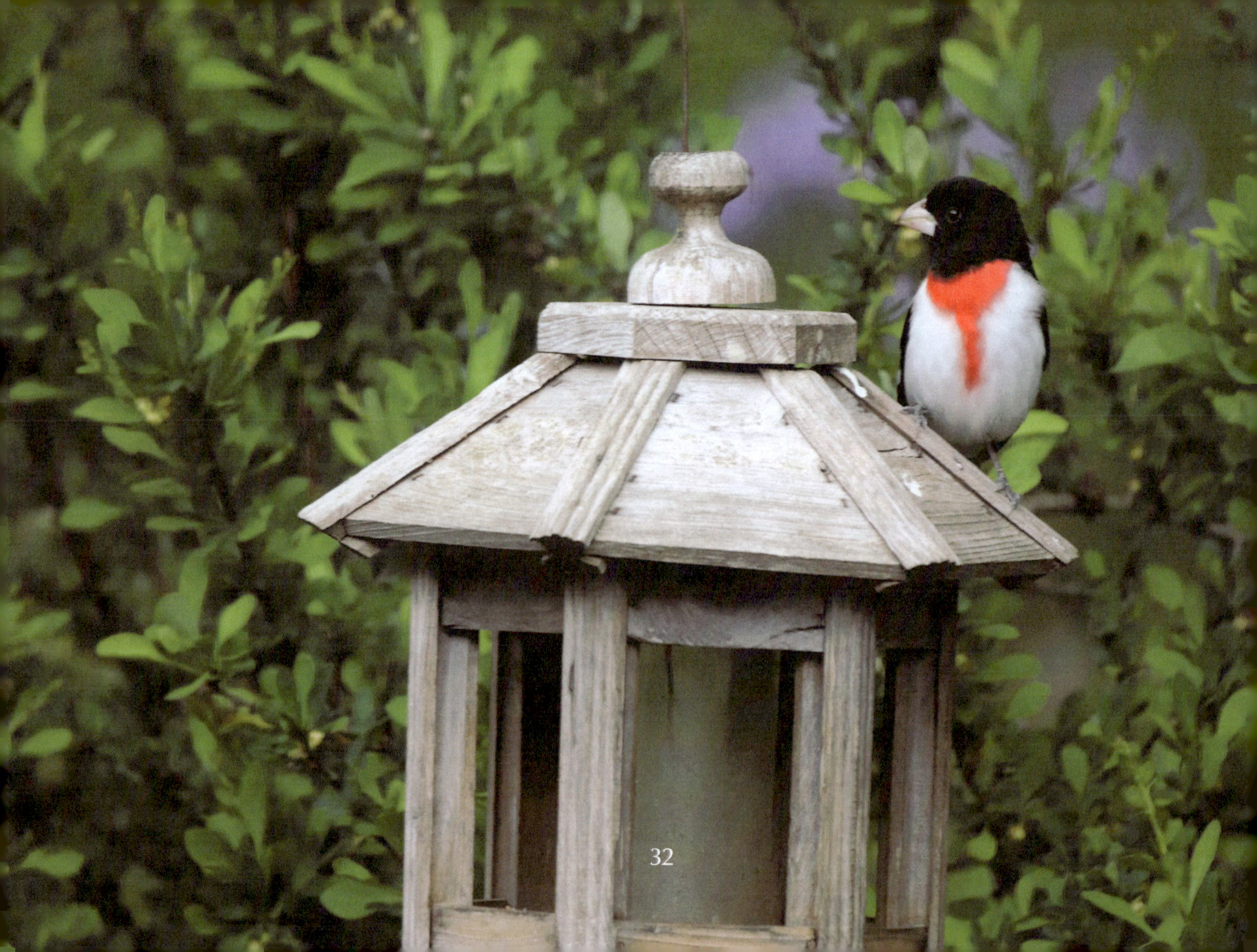

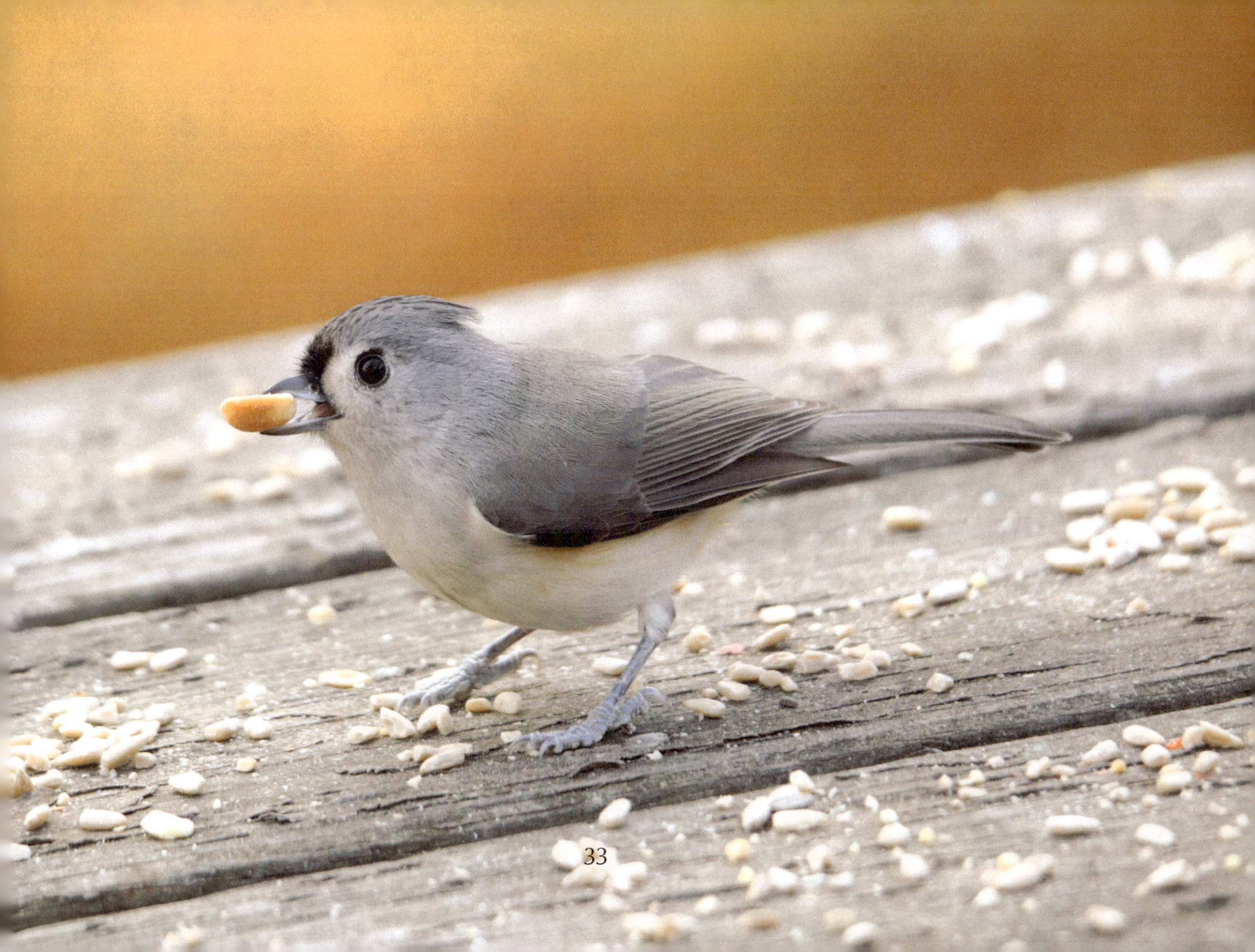

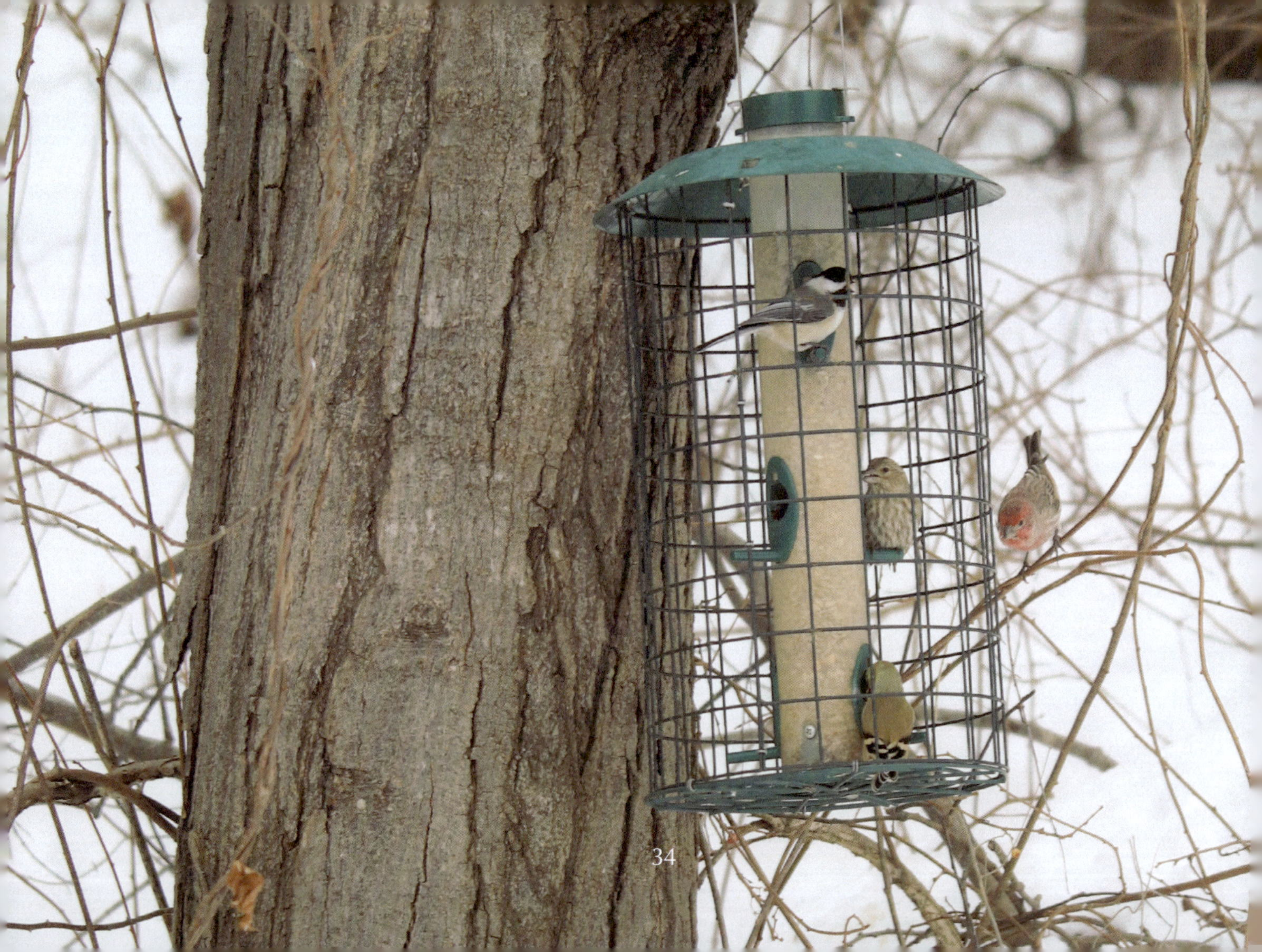

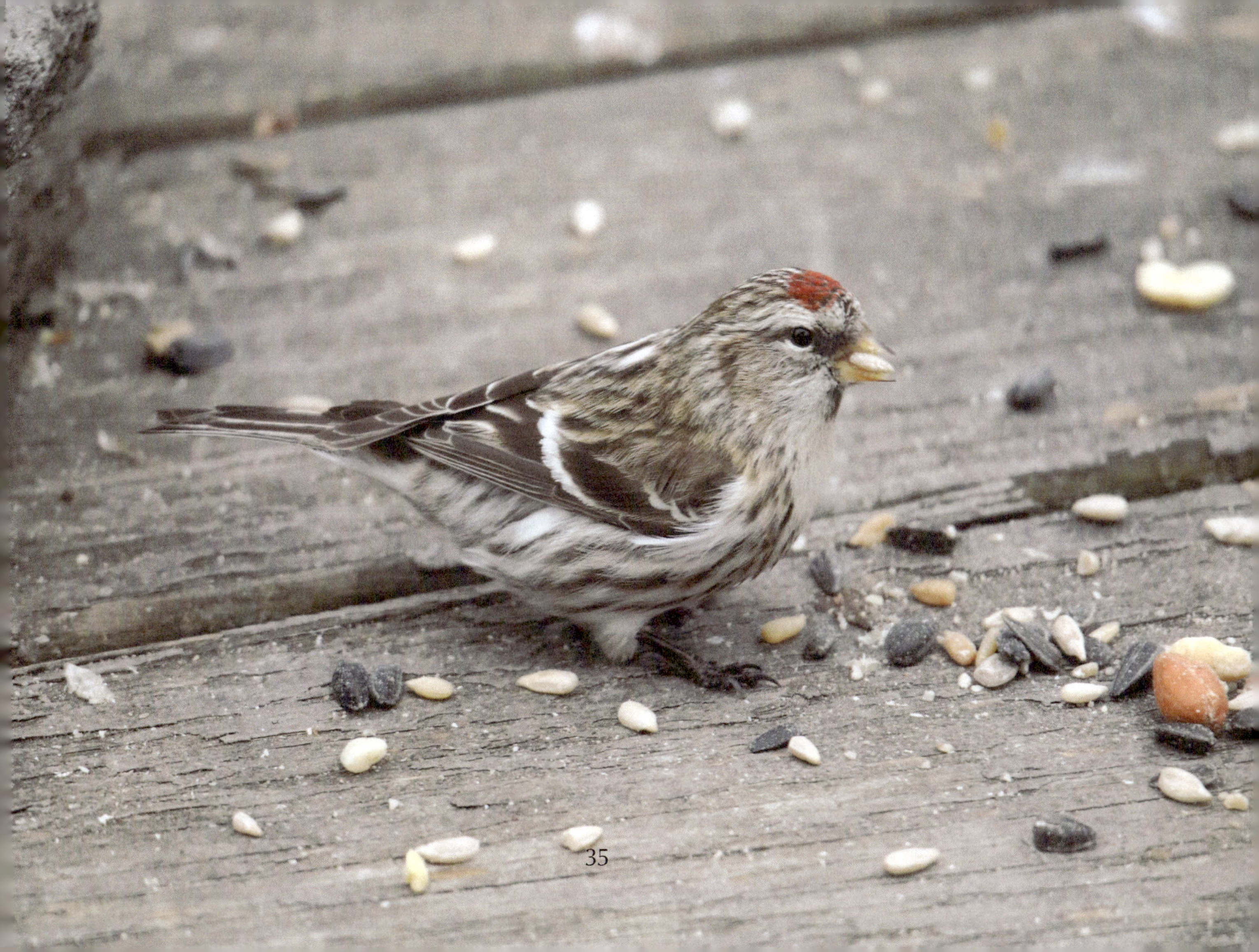

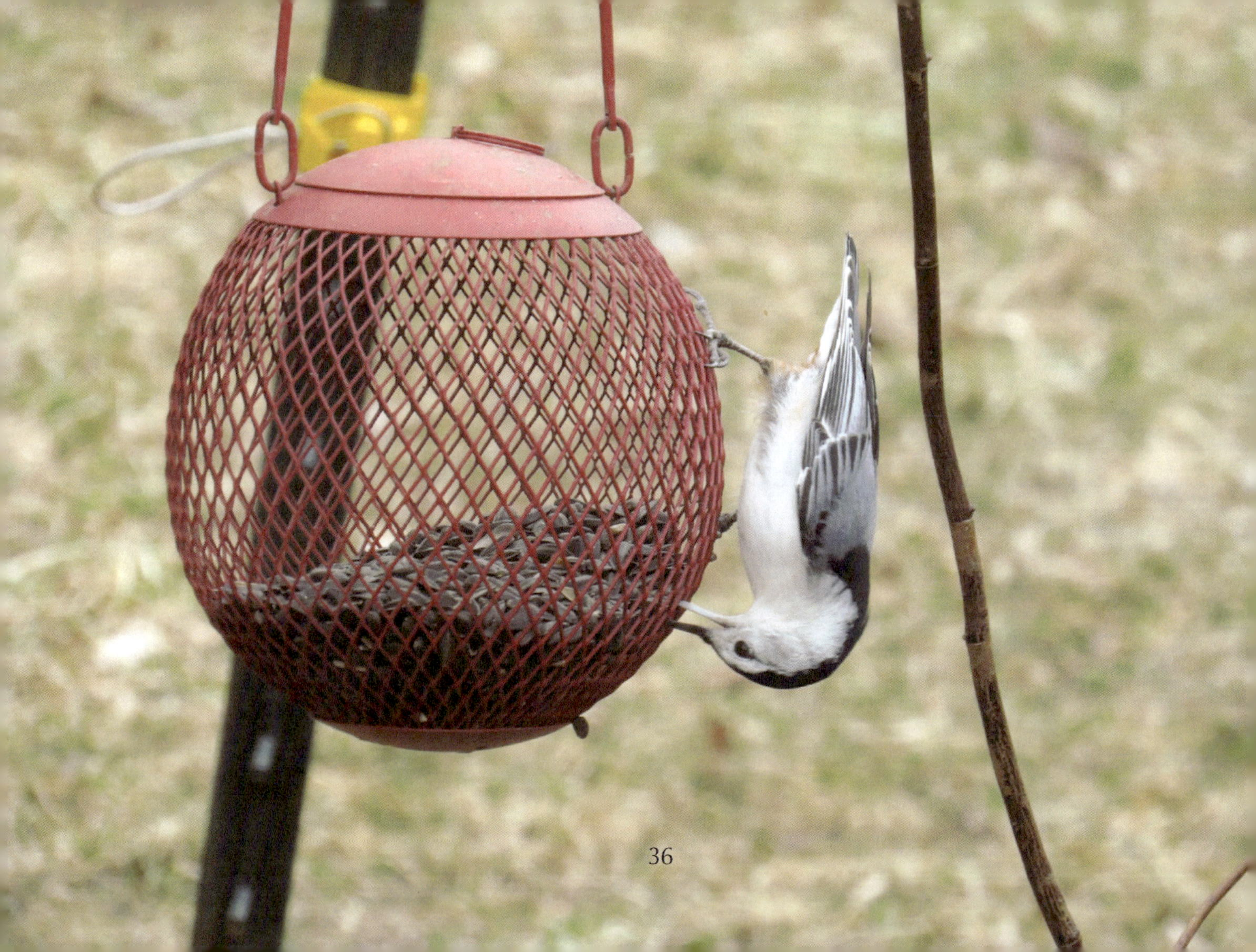

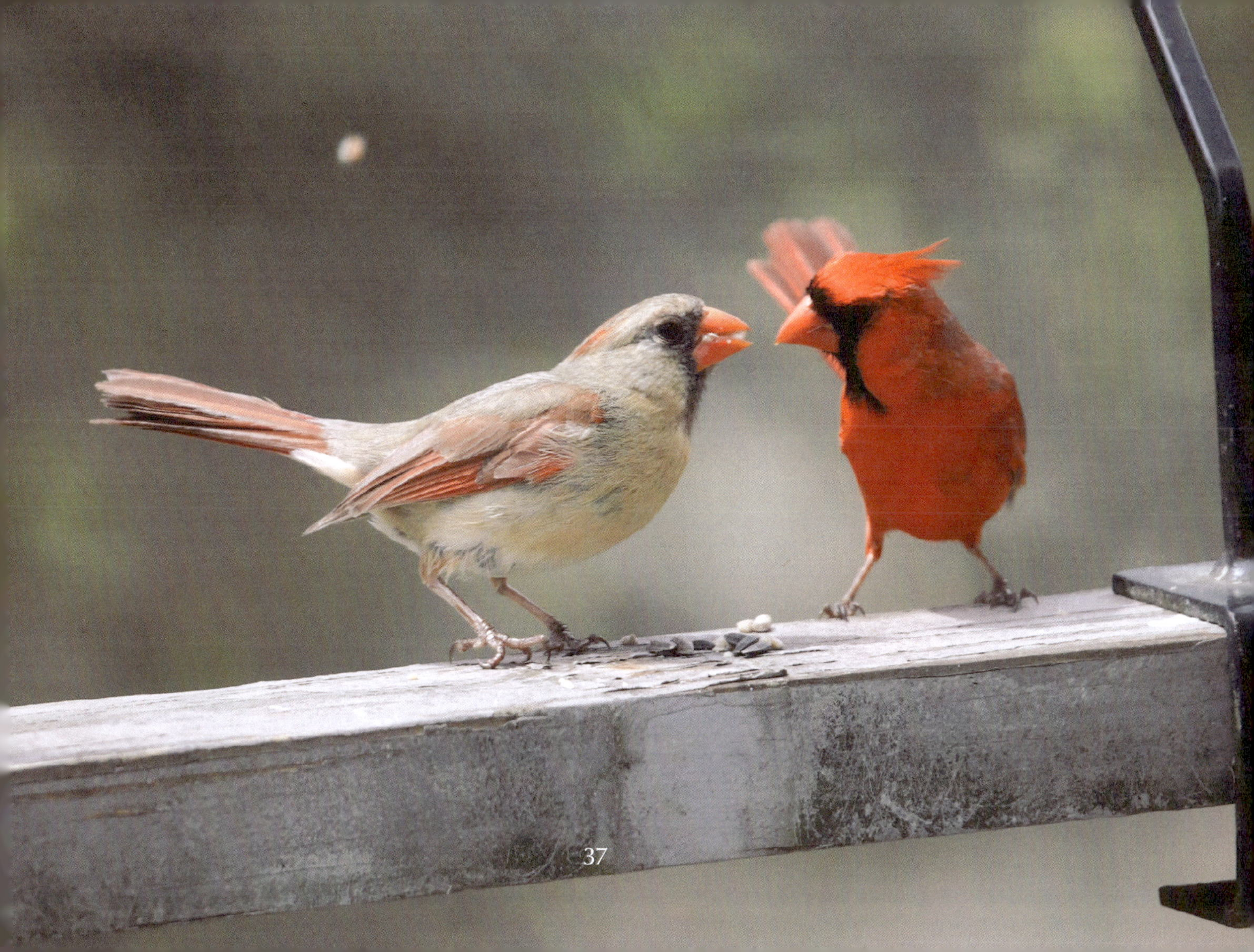

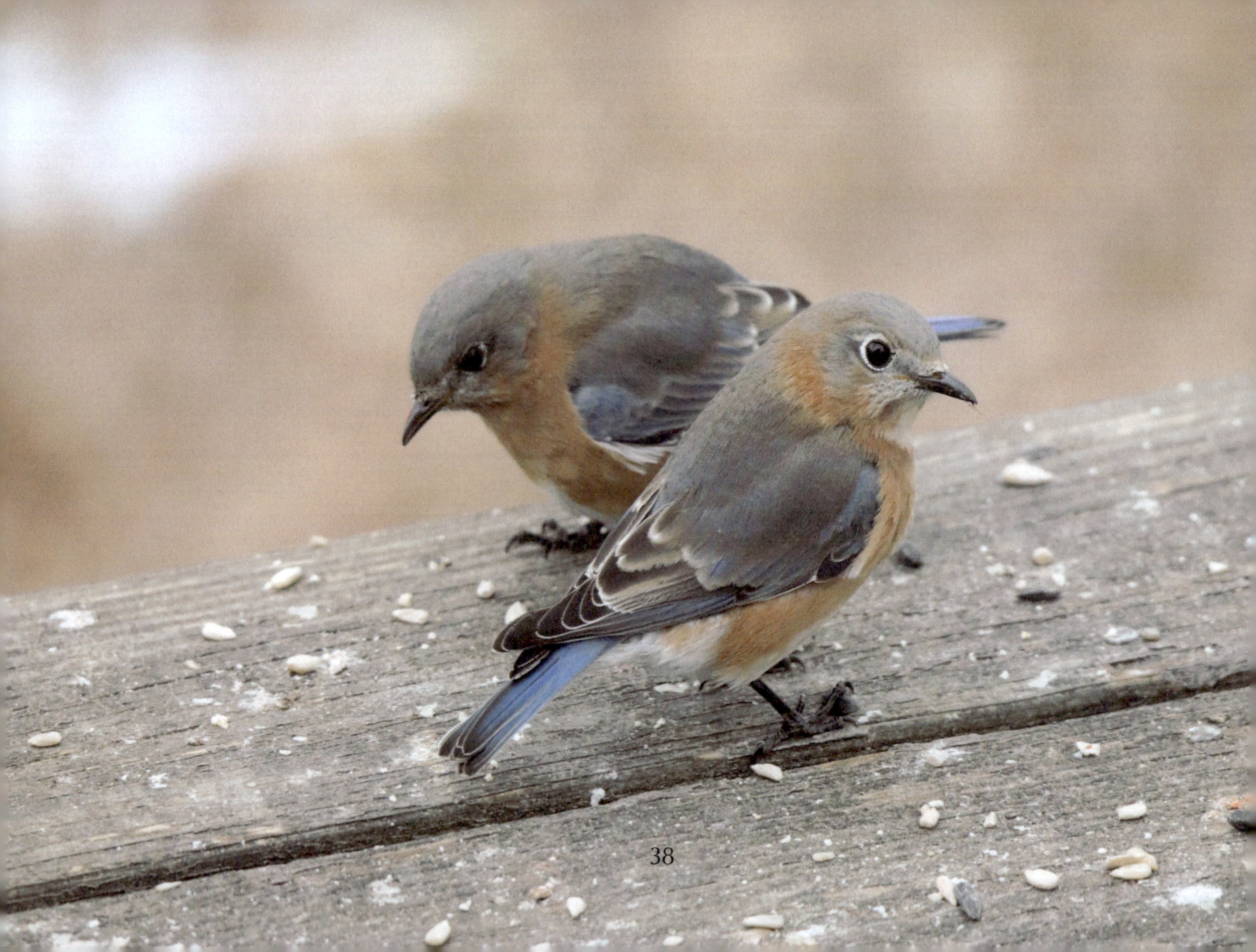

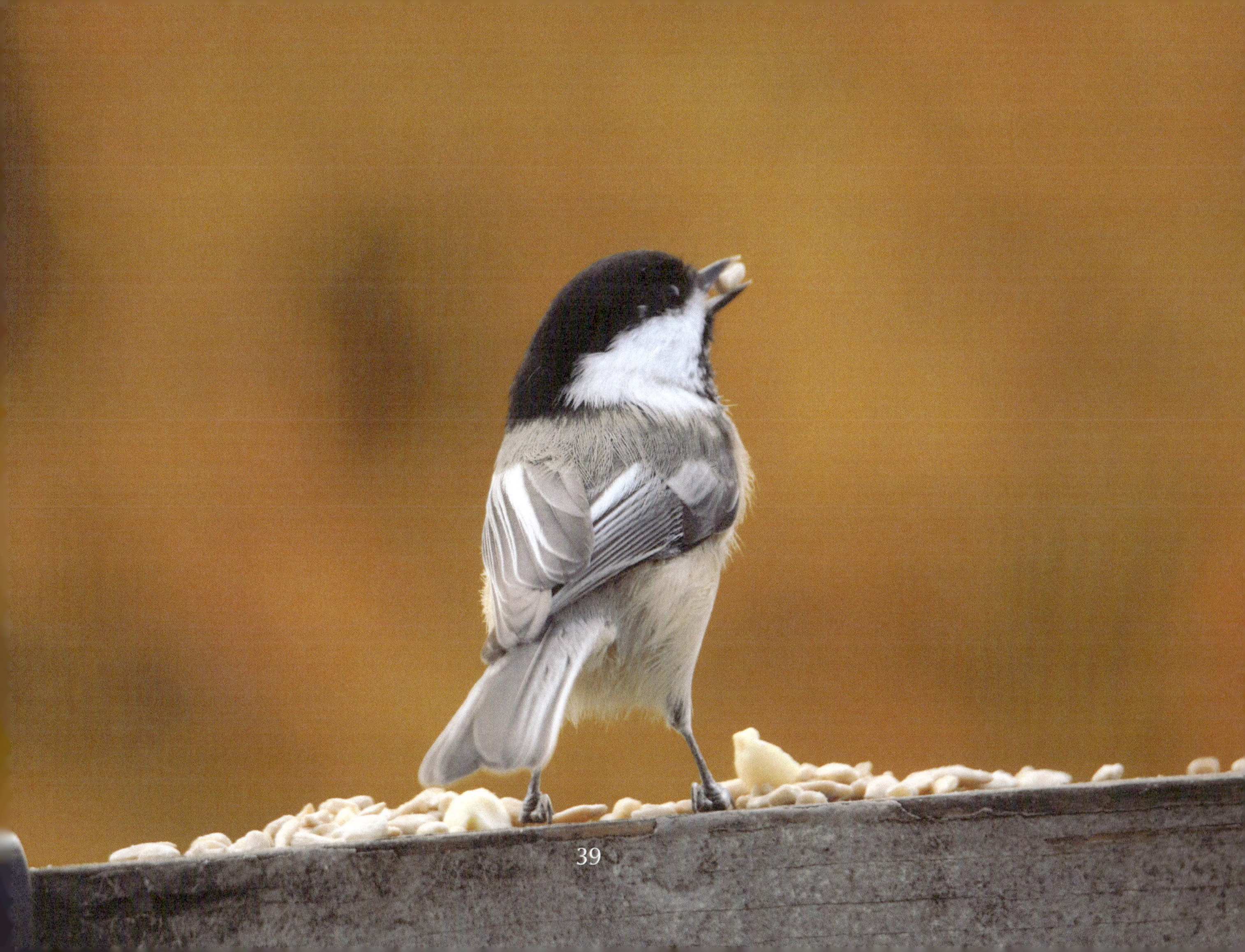

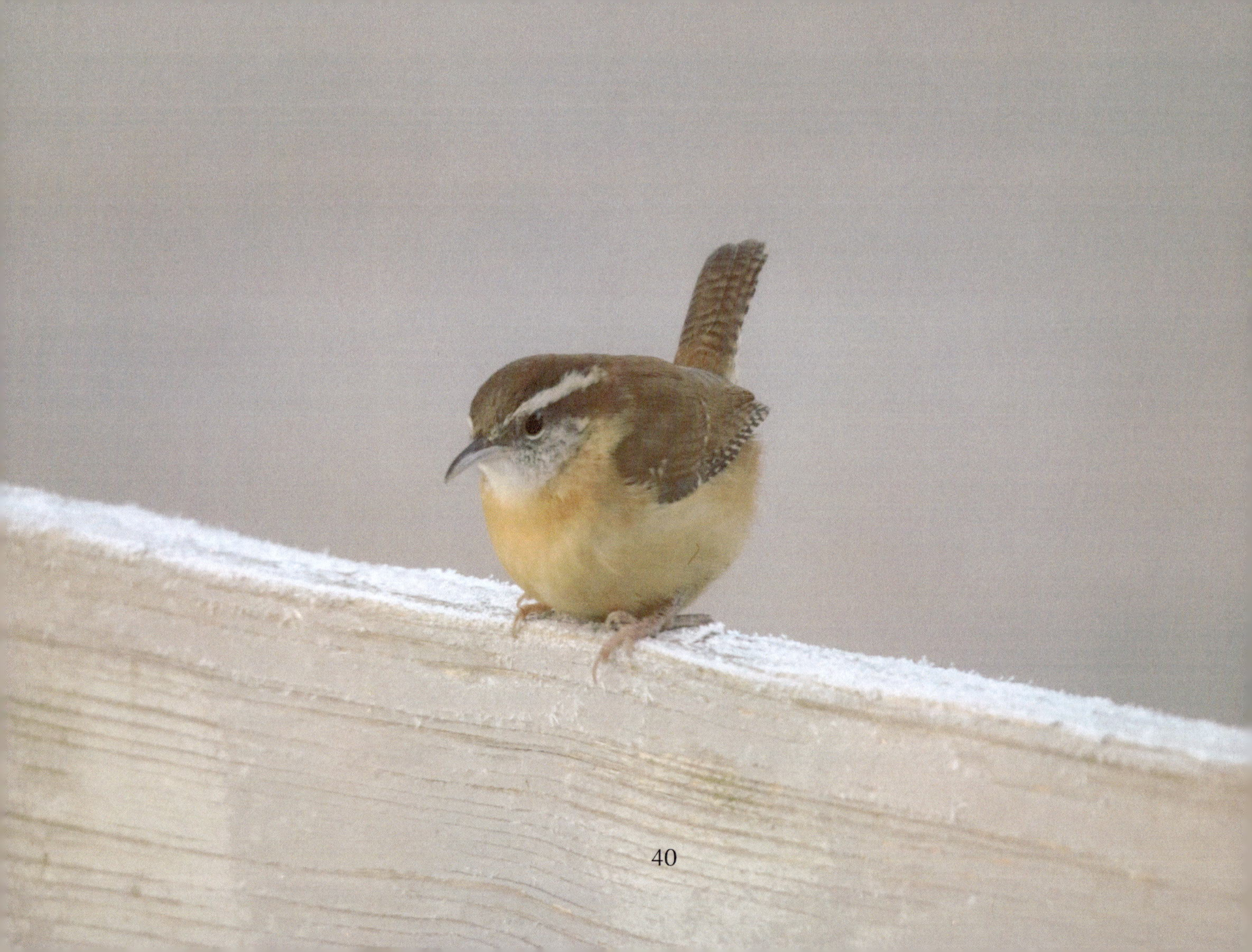

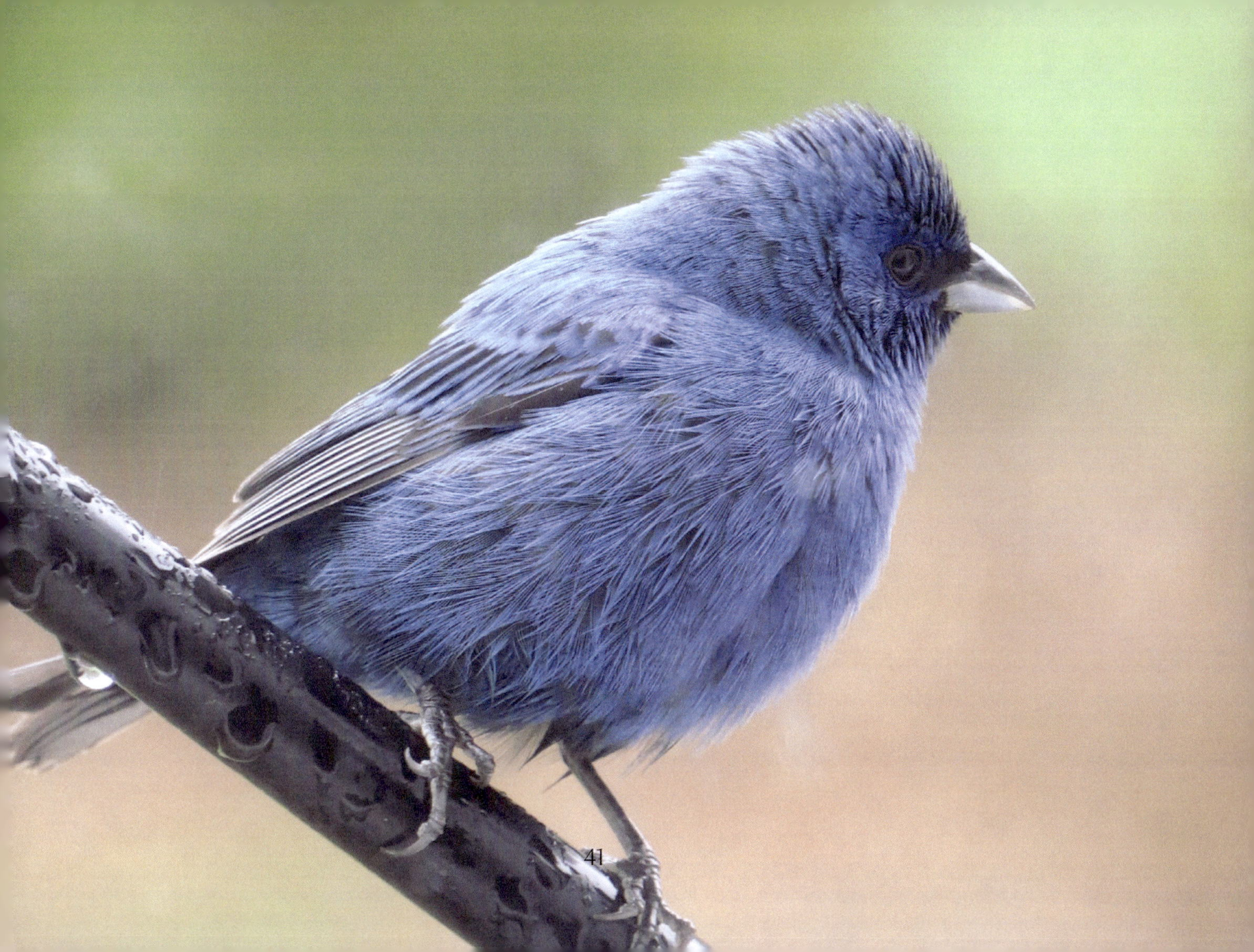

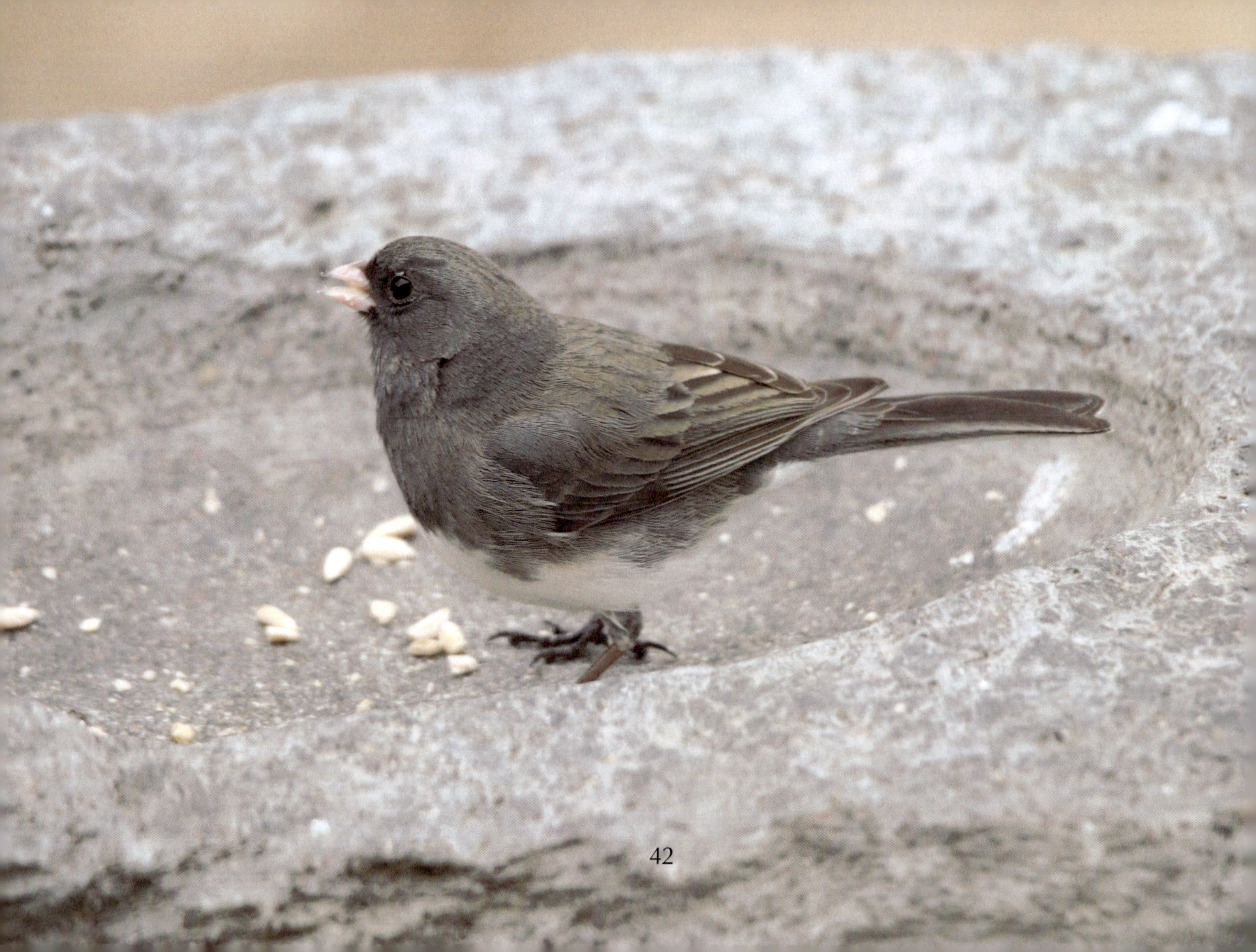

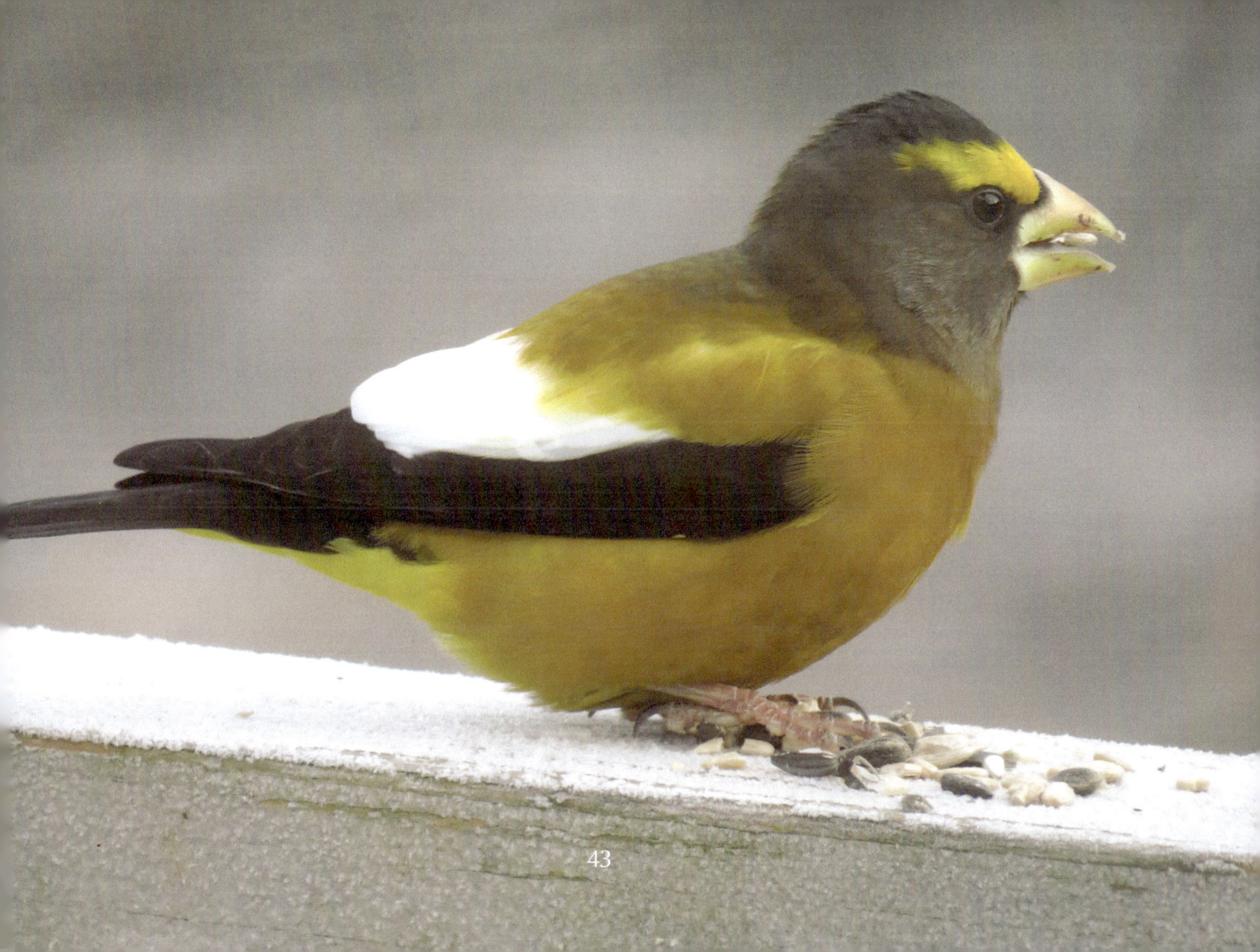

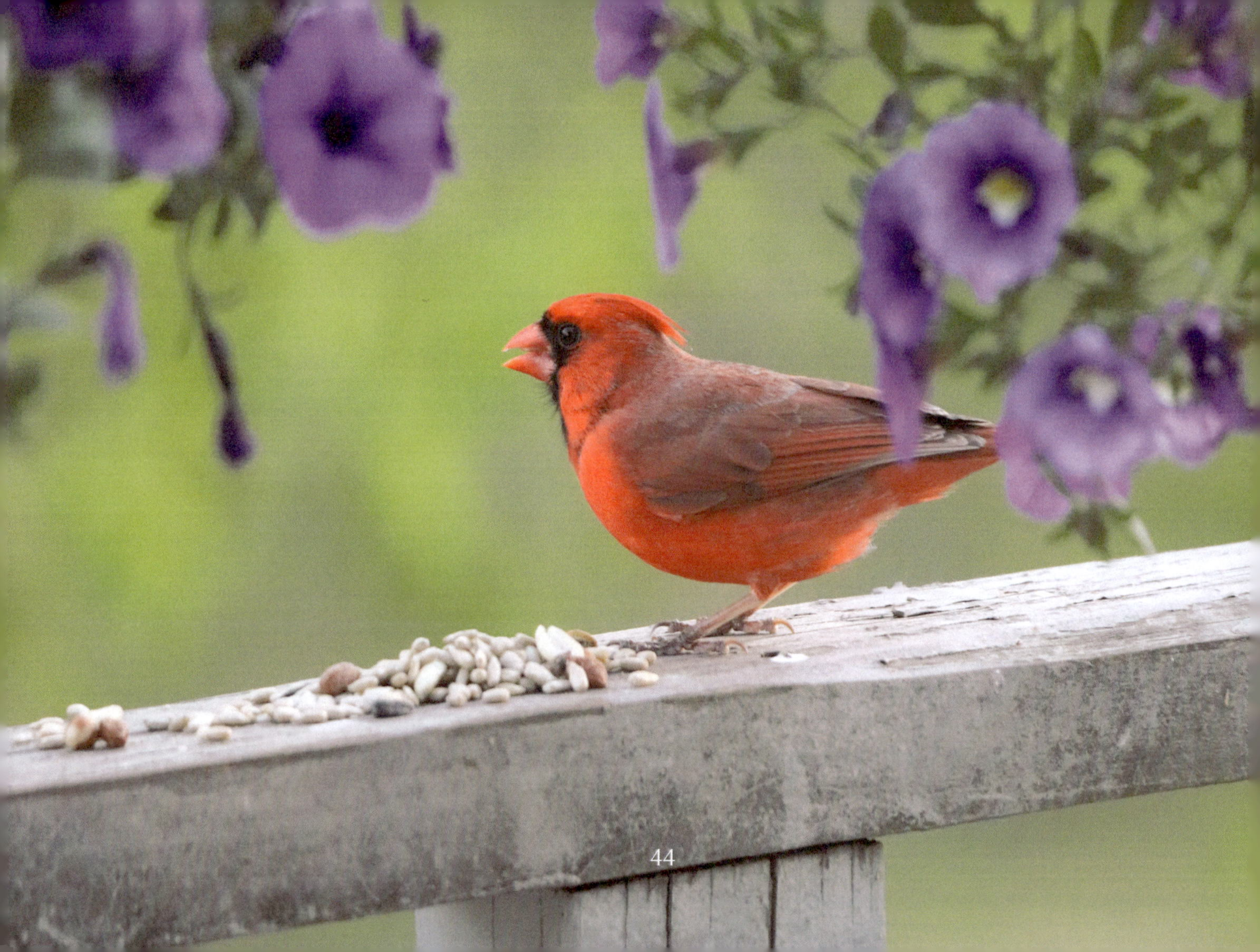

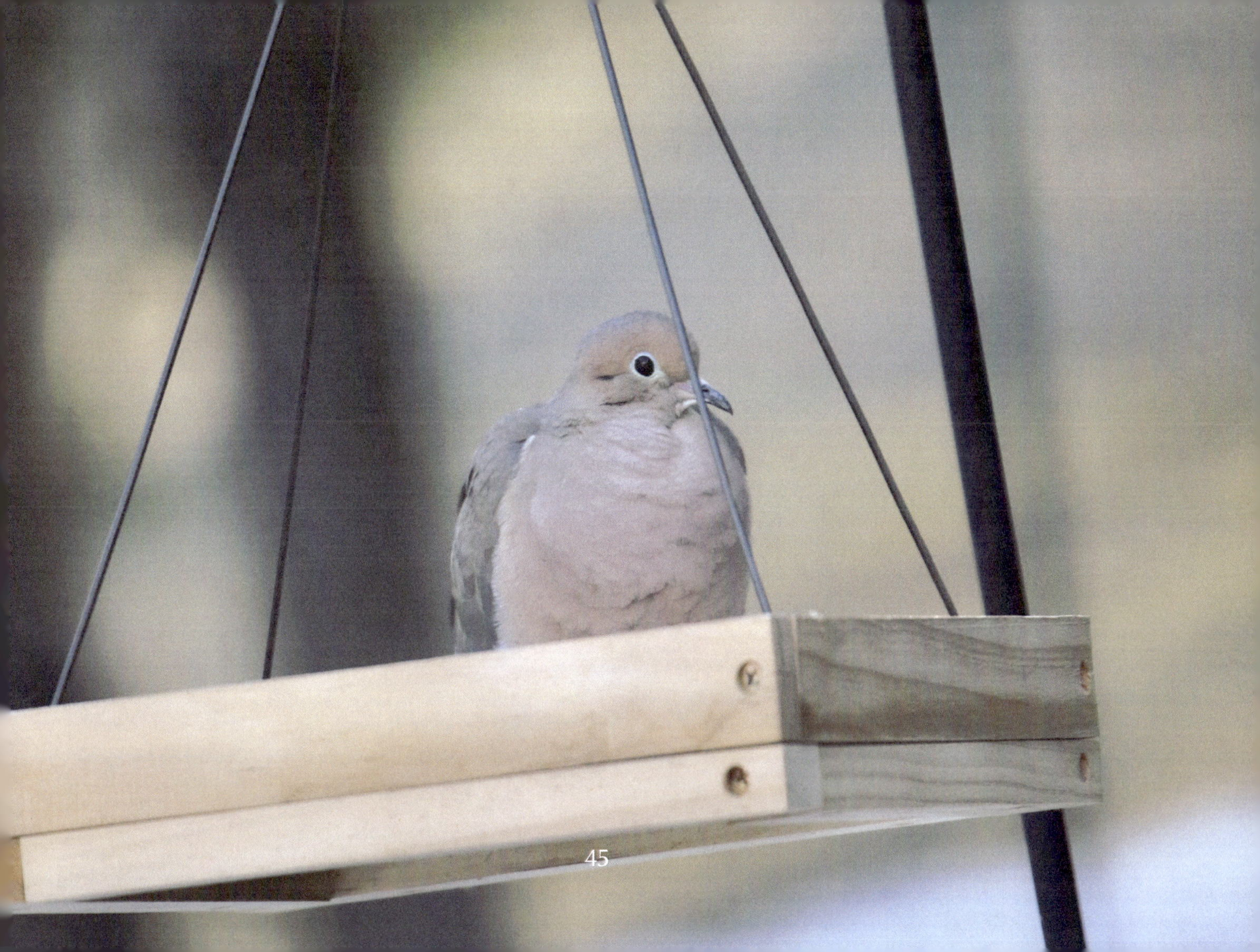

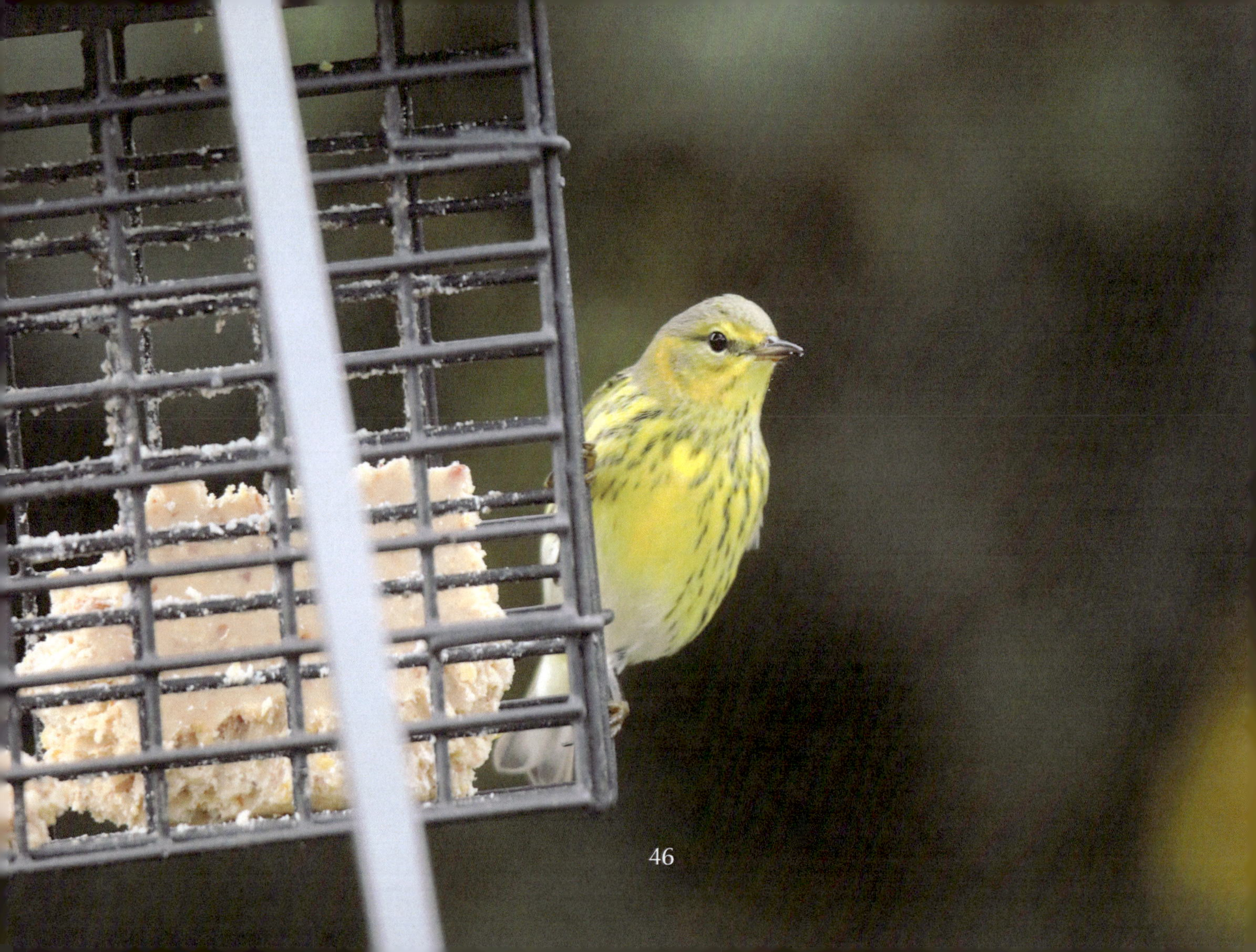

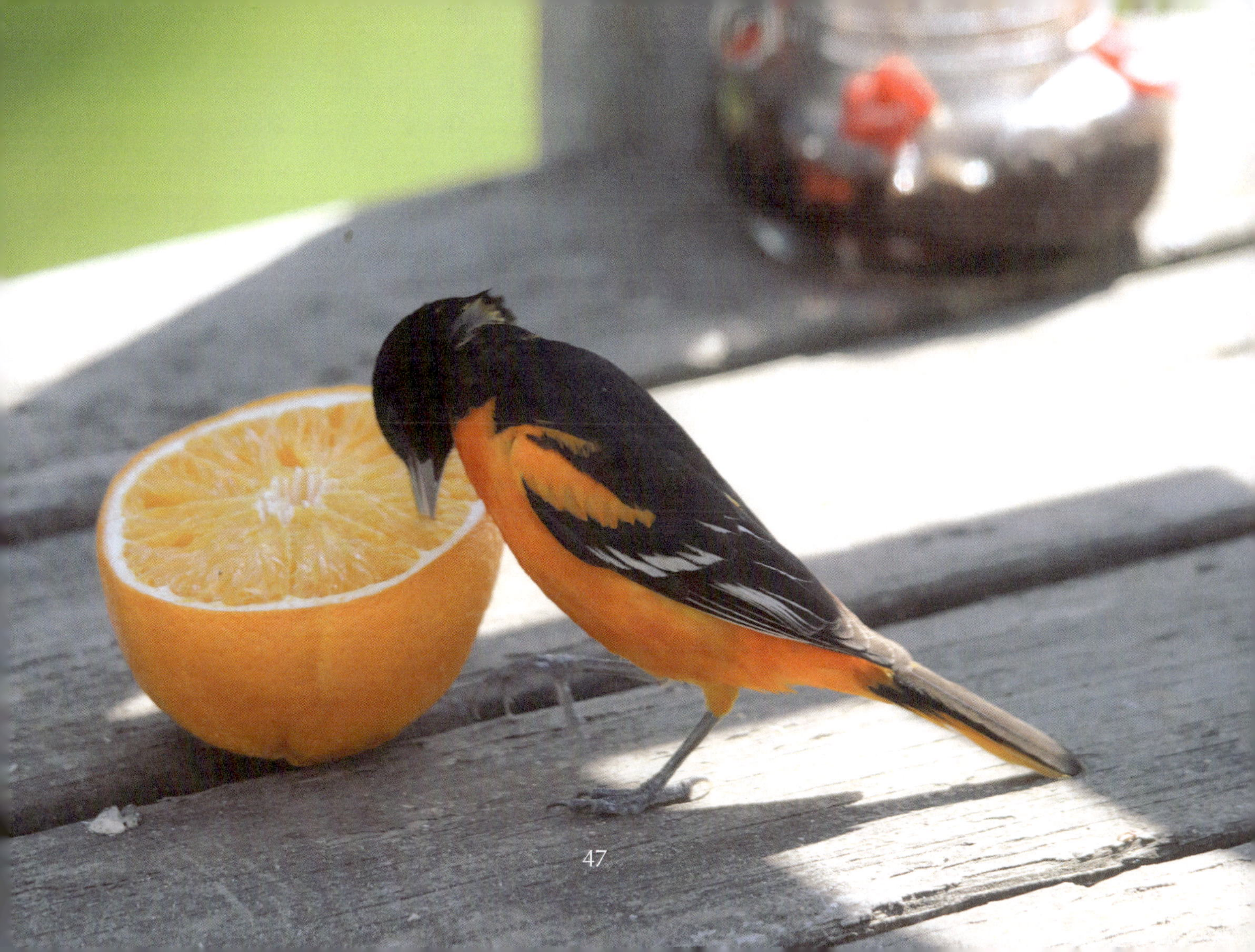

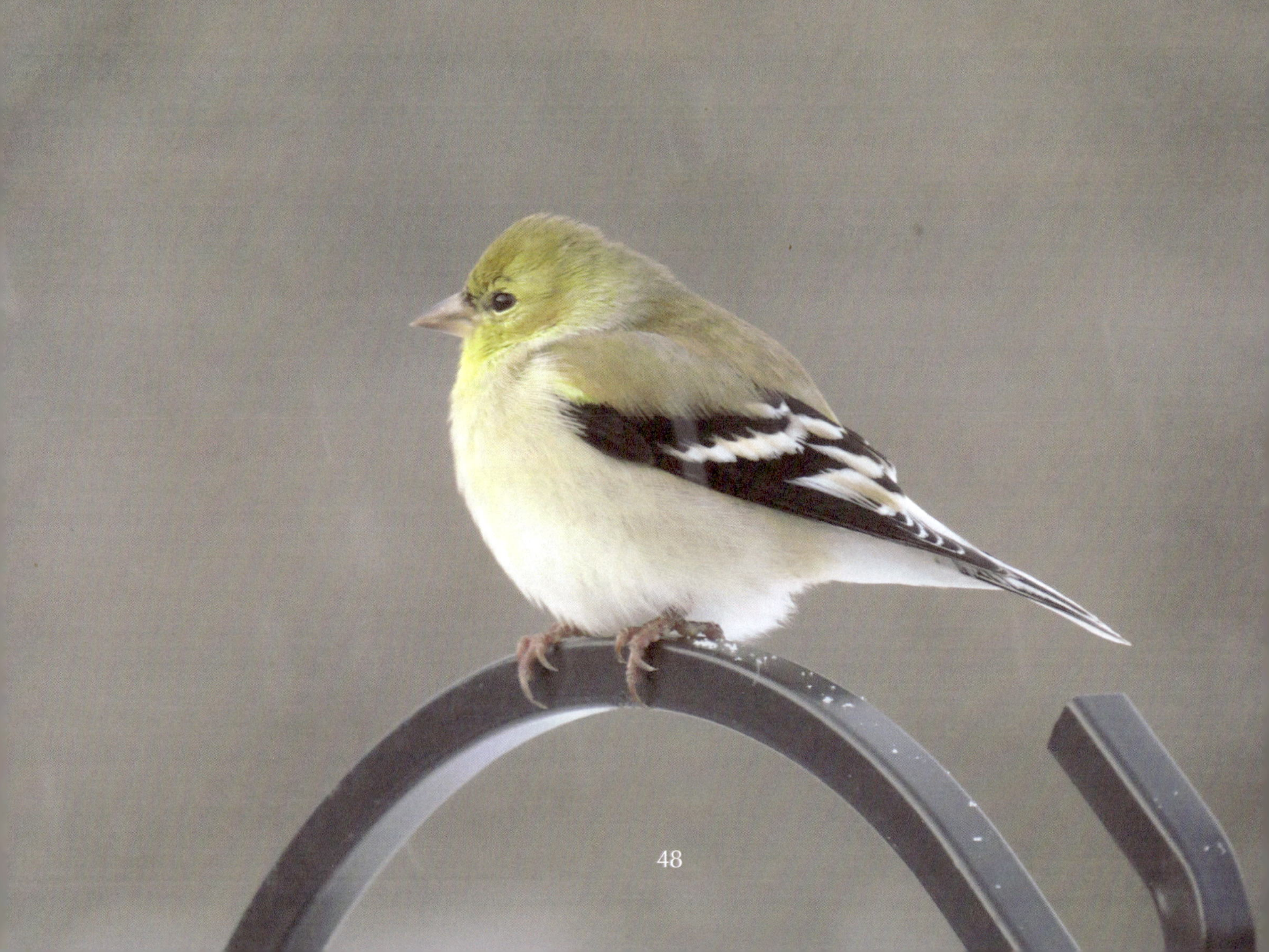

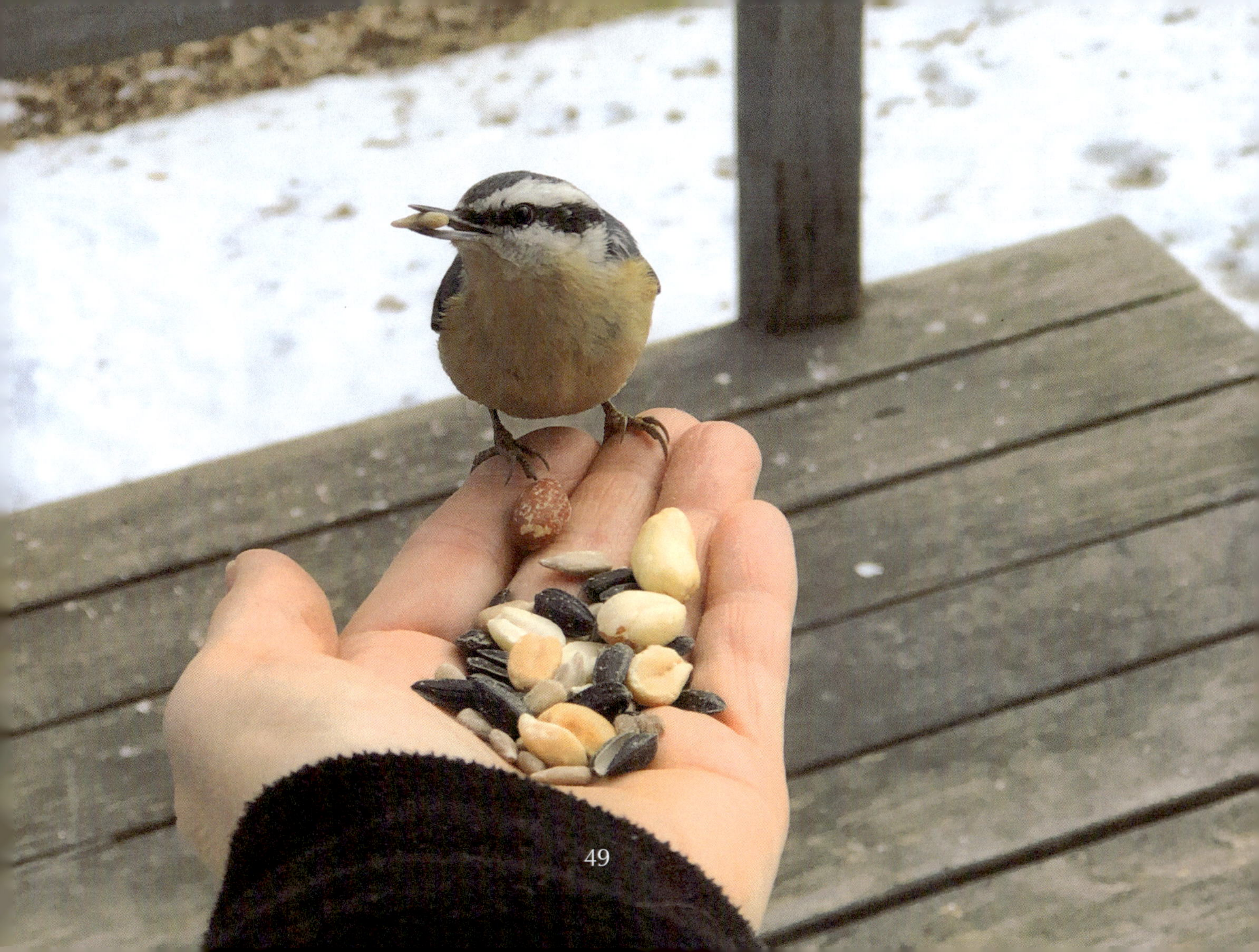

Index of Bird Names

www.ingramcontent.com/pod-product-compliance
Lightning Source LLC
Chambersburg PA
CBRC100833110726
48006CB00009B/1388